This book is dedicated to Russ Jolley
and to Donald and Elizabeth Lawrence,
who were studying and working to protect
Mount St. Helens and the Columbia Gorge
back when most of us now active were
still wearing three-cornered pants.

Mount St. Helens and Spirit Lake from Harmony Trail 224

MOUNT ST. HELENS
NATIONAL VOLCANIC MONUMENT

A Pocket Guide for
Hikers, Viewers, and Skiers

By Chuck Williams

The Mountaineers
Seattle

THE MOUNTAINEERS: Organized 1906 "...to explore, study, preserve and enjoy the natural beauty of the Northwest."

© 1988 by Chuck Willams
All rights reserved

Published by: The Mountaineers
 306 Second Avenue West, Seattle, Washington 98119

Manufactured in the United States of America

Edited by Cathy Johnson
Maps by Ann Alexander and Gary Rands
Designed by Chuck Williams
Produced by Elephant Mountain Arts, White Salmon
All photographs by the author unless otherwise credited
Cover: Mount St. Helens and Spirit Lake from Norway Pass
Title page: Mount St. Helens' crater and Mount Hood
Bear grass drawing (opposite page) by Liz Smith

4 3 2 1 0
5 4 3 2

Library of Congress Cataloging-in-Publication Data

Williams, Chuck. 1943-
    Mount St. Helens National Volcanic Monument: a pocket guide for hikers, viewers, and skiers / by Chuck Williams.
        p. cm.
    Includes index.
    ISBN 0-89886-078-4 (pbk.)
    1. Mount St. Helens National Volcanic Monument (Wash.)—Guide
-books. I. Title. II. Title: Mount St. Helens National Volcanic
Monument.
F897.S17W55 1988
917.97'84—dc19   88-19036
                                                               CIP

CONTENTS

NOTE: This guide is written to be used in conjunction with the U.S. Forest Service's map entitled *Mount St. Helens National Volcanic Monument*, as well as such Mountaineers guides as *100 Hikes in the South Cascades and Olympics* and *Trips and Trails, 2.* The Forest Service may change some trail numbers, so trail numbers at trailheads may not always be the same as in this book.

PREFACE

Mount St. Helens' youthful, Fuji-like symmetry stood out among the older, more-weathered peaks of the Cascade Range. Especially in winter, with a glistening white coat of snow, the mountain hovered above the dark evergreen horizon like a mirage, too perfect to exist except in our minds. Even so, Mount St. Helens was overshadowed by other Cascade Range volcanoes—until it suddenly became active again in 1980.

Before it reawakened, little had been done to protect Mount St. Helens, in part because it is smaller than many of the Cascade volcanoes, such as Mount Rainier to the north. Much of the landscape surrounding Mount St. Helens was devastated by clearcut logging before the 1980 eruptions; only Spirit Lake and Mount Margaret on the north side—the main target of the blast—were still in a seminatural state. And the chainsaws were closing in on that beautiful basin.

A major eruptive cycle began in March 1980, and two months later a tremendous explosion blew the top off Mount St. Helens, resculptured Spirit Lake, and spread ash across the land. A jagged, rapidly changing crater replaced the oval, glacier-topped crown. The surrounding landscape was suddenly and dramatically changed.

"People can protect wilderness, but only Nature can create it," goes a truism in the environmental movement. Mount St. Helens' May 18, 1980, eruption created new wilderness out of developed areas in a matter of minutes. The "devastated" area is rapidly becoming covered with wildflowers and other plants, and animals have moved back to the volcano's slopes. Large evergreens will someday return, too, continuing the cycle. Meanwhile, this is a fascinating landscape—a barren one that is still alien and unworldly to most visitors.

Congress established a Mount St. Helens National Volcanic Monument in 1982, but conservationists considered the legislation less than ideal. It included only half the acreage wanted by environmental groups and did not make the active volcano a national park, as was done with other volcanoes that erupted this century; the legislation left management with the U.S. Forest Service. The mountain, however, will continue to have the last word.

Mount St. Helens will erupt again in the years and centuries to come, and the present landscape will evolve into lush forests and meadows—and then back to dust and ash, and on and on. Eventually, the volcano will become dormant and be worn down by water and ice.

Visitors to Mount St. Helens National Volcanic Monument can witness firsthand the processes that created much of the Pacific Northwest's beauty. Unlike most wilderness areas and parks, which generally change less than any other places in the country, the landscape around Mount St. Helens is changing rapidly, still noticeable from year to year. I hope this guide will help you enjoy visits to the active volcano, as well as better understand the natural forces at work.

— *Chuck Williams*

1. A YOUNG, ACTIVE VOLCANO

The cycle of eruptions at Mount St. Helens tha
began in 1980 was not really unexpected. Noting it
"long history of spasmodic explosive activity," govern
ment geologists familiar with Mount St. Helens ha
written that it was "probably the volcano most likel
to endanger people and property in the western Unite
States." They had predicted an eruption before the en
of the century, but had found little public or govern
mental interest in the warnings. The Cascade Range i
a chain of volcanoes, many of them still semiactive, s
eruptions are inevitable. In fact, the current period o
relative calm may be abnormal.

Crater and lava
dome in 1982

Ring Of Fire

The perimeter of the Pacific Ocean is dotted with volcanoes, the "Ring of Fire." Scientists now think that the earth's surface is composed of huge tectonic plates above partly molten rock, and that the plates below the Pacific are expanding, forcing themselves beneath the surrounding continental plates. The crust being forced down into the earth's hot mantle melts, turning into magma, which works itself up through fissures in the plates, forming mountains such as the Cascade Range. When gases in the magma build up pressure below the surface, it is released through explosive volcanic eruptions.

Mount St. Helens is a young volcano, an adolescent, and its unique symmetry prior to the 1980 eruption was primarily a result of its youth. The older volcanic cones in the Cascade Range were buried beneath glaciers during recent ice ages, and the rivers of ice gouged and reshaped the peaks' soft silhouettes. Since Mount St. Helens' upper cone emerged long after the last ice age retreated, glaciers and other erosive forces had only begun to sculpt it before it was blown away in 1980.

Although it emerged atop an older volcano, which dates back some 40,000 years, the visible cone is thought to have formed within the last 2500 years, long after people were living in the region. In fact, the upper cone was only a few hundred years old.

Even now-peaceful lakes around Mount St. Helens were born of geologic violence. Spirit Lake formed when mudflows from the volcano blocked the headwaters of a fork of the Toutle River, and the level of the lake was raised over 60 feet by mudflows about 1500 A.D.

Unlike most other Cascade volcanoes, which are famed for their wildflower displays, Mount St. Helens had virtually no alpine meadows even before the 1980 eruption. And timberline on the mountain was usually

AT BOYS CAMP-MT.ST.HELENS.   SPIRIT LAKE, WASH. A76.

only about 4000 feet above sea-level, more than 2000 feet below what is normal at this latitude. Few plants can colonize the recent pumice since it doesn't retain moisture. Merrill Lake and some of the mountain's glaciers don't even have outlet streams; the water seeps into the pumice and emerges elsewhere as springs.

Geologist Jean Verhoogen and botanist Dr. Donald B. Lawrence began studying Mount St. Helens in the 1930s and soon realized how recent the volcano had been active. The mountain's low timberline intrigued Lawrence, and by analyzing tree rings, which show less growth following eruptions, he concluded that there had been a major ash and pumice eruption about 1802.

Other research followed, including by U.S. Geological Survey scientists Donal Mullineaux and Dwight Crandell, and the scientific community began to realize how active—and potentially dangerous—the beautiful mountain was. Their warnings were not heeded, however.

Born Again

Mount St. Helens' 1980 eruption cycle began on March 20, when scientists recorded a strong earthquake near the mountain. For the next week, the earthquakes increased rapidly, arriving in swarms.

Then on March 27, a loud boom announced the first eruption. A cloud of steam and ash rose high into the sky, and a small crater—about 250 feet wide—opened atop the awakening mountain. A second opening soon appeared, and the two craters kept enlarging until they merged into one large hole about 1700 feet across and 850 feet deep. Mount St. Helens was fairly calm during April, although there were minor eruptions and harmonic tremors, vibrations thought to be caused by magma moving deep beneath the volcano.

By early May, however, the area around The Boot, a protrusion where climbers on Mountaineers outings had once warmed themselves near hot spots, was bulging out at a rate of five feet per day. As the north side swelled, Goat Rocks, a dacite dome and debris fan created by the 1842-44 eruptions, moved more than 300 feet out. Steam and ash eruptions began anew. The top of the volcano started coming apart, and huge cracks appeared. The south side of the summit remained stable, but the north side moved outward and down. Mount St. Helens was literally bursting at the seams.

Then on the morning of May 18, 1980, an earthquake triggered a massive landslide; much of the north face slid down the mountain. With the confining weight—the lid on the volcano—gone, a tremendous lateral blast overtook the landslide and devastated everything in its path. Next, the summit exploded, sending an ash plume more than 60,000 feet into the air, blocking the sunlight.

The lateral blast and avalanches of hot gases and rock debris leveled all trees for 17 miles to the northeast.

The intense heat scorched many more. Mudflows, fueled by the melting snow and ice, caused extensive flooding, especially along the Toutle River, whose temperature rose to above 100° F. Spirit Lake was enlarged and turned into a mudhole. The blast blew water out of some lakes and killed large numbers of fish and birds, the mountain's goats and ptarmigans, thousands of deer and elk, and dozens of people. Falling ash immobilized life for hundreds of miles to the northeast, and the ominous ash-cloud drifted around the world.

The eruptions diminished over the next few days, but on May 27, another major eruption filled the sky. Then on June 12, when the winds had changed, the ash from yet another huge eruption covered Portland and western Washington. A lava dome formed in the crater, but it was blown away by an eruption. More eruptions, large and small, followed sporadically. A new lava dome is now filling the 1900-foot-deep crater.

U.S. Geological Survey scientists, who had studied the volcano for decades, wrote in 1978 that "future eruptions of Mount St. Helens are a near certainty" and "it will not be possible to prevent, or to stop them after they have begun." Their statements are still true.

Dust To Moss, Ashes To Trees

Until Mount St. Helens has another major eruption, the landscape around the volcano will increasingly turn green and be full of life. In fact, the quick reappearance of plants and animals in the once-barren blast zone has been as amazing as the radical changes caused by the 1980 eruption. Islands of life that survived are spreading and merging, greatly aiding the recolonization of the blast zone. As is Nature's way, the death of some living things is helping give birth to new living things. Researchers in the blast zone found elk bones with a patch of wildflowers in the shape of the former carcass.

Within three years, more than 230 plant species, over ninety percent of those previously found at Mount St. Helens, had returned, but in lesser numbers. However, different species now dominate. For example, understory plants are now thriving instead of Douglas fir.

Plants like huckleberries sprouted from roots that survived the blast, others grew from seeds blown into the blast zone. Pioneer plants, such as fireweed, lupine, and pearly everlasting, quickly colonized the blast zone, making it possible for other plants to follow, especially on the nitrogen-poor pyroclastic flows. Erosion is still exposing more soil, helping plantlife to recover.

Pocket gophers survived underground and were able to survive on roots. Now they are helping, not harming, plantlife; their burrowing mixes pumice with soil, and their mounds make good seed beds. Elk returned within weeks, and scientists soon trapped weasels, raccoons, and chipmunks on the pumice plain in front of the crater. These mammals bring in more seeds, and their scat provides nutrients for plants. The forests of snags have attracted pileated woodpeckers and mountain bluebirds, but animals requiring old-growth forest, such as spotted owls and flying squirrels, are not yet coming back.

Spirit Lake has gone through radical changes because of the 1980 eruptions. A day after the May 18 blast, the temperature of the lake once known for its cold water was 91°F (33°C). A "primordial soup" formed as bacteria and microscopic organisms fed on the rich organic materials that filled the lake. Decomposing bacteria quickly depleted the oxygen in the lake, creating an anaerobic environment that gave off a bad smell the first summer following the 1980 eruption. Due to the lack of predation, the usually microscopic organisms grow large enough here to be seen with the naked eye. Salamanders and frogs survived up side creeks and are returning to the lake. Killdeer and hummingbirds have come back.

Fish were killed in waters near the volcano, but lakes in the Mount Margaret backcountry were covered with snow and ice, so most fish and zooplackton survived and are replenishing streams hurt by mudflows. Scientists got a five-year moratorium on the state's stocking of fish at the Monument so that their research would not be adversely affected, but the ban is expiring.

About half of the blast zone was salvage-logged, but the portion within the Monument has provided scientists with valuable new information about plant and animal succession following natural disturbances. Most surprising has been the important role of surviving organisms in spreading new life. And in coming years, much more will be learned from the 1980 eruption of Mount St. Helens.

15

In 1916 the U.S. Forest Service constructed a fire lookout atop the volcano, using mules to carry materials to the summit. After a decade, however, the lookout was boarded up, because it was usually in clouds and thus was a better warming hut for climbers than a fire lookout.

2. THE HUMAN SIDE OF THE RESTLESS MOUNTAIN

Mount St. Helens is a young, active volcano and thus has discouraged nearby human settlement. Local Indians evidently avoided the upper slopes of Mount St. Helens, which was fairly active until the mid-1800s. When Canadian painter Paul Kane traveled through the Northwest in 1847, he drew eruptions from the Columbia and Cowlitz rivers, but was unable to find an Indian guide who would take him to Spirit Lake and the volcano.

Tribes in the vicinity of Mount St. Helens used the area around the volcano seasonally. Each had its own name for the peak and its own legends regarding the mountain's history. Loowit is now a commonly used "Indian" name for the volcano.

Loowit, or Mount St. Helens, had been quiet for more than a century before the 1980 eruptions, and people, beginning with miners and loggers, had settled into the Spirit Lake basin and along its outlet, the North Fork Toutle River. Those interested in recreation and tourism soon followed. During the decades immediately preceding the new eruptive phase, Mount St. Helens was increasingly developed, including clearcuts far up its slopes.

Now, however, as it was until a century ago, no one lives on the volcano, not even in the formerly wooded Spirit Lake basin. More and more of the area, however, is being opened to visitors, providing hikers thrilling opportunities to explore a newly formed landscape, one that now demands far more respect from us than it previously did.

Legendary Mountain

Mount St. Helens rose in a rugged, sparsely used land between three diverse prehistoric cultures: the Salish-speaking people of Puget Sound and what was to become northern Washington, the Sahaptin-speaking tribes of the plateau east of the Cascades, and the Chinookan-speaking residents of the lower Columbia River.

The peoples known as the Cowlitz Indians, though politically united, were actually two distinct groups. The residents along the lower and middle Cowlitz River were Coast Salish, while the Taidnapam, or Upper Cowlitz, who lived directly north and south of the volcano, increasingly spoke Sahaptin, although Salish culture and bloodlines continued to dominate. The Klicki-tat Indians, whose territory included the high prairies between Mount St. Helens, Mount Adams, and the Columbia River Gorge, spoke Sahaptin and culturally were closely related to the Yakima people.

The natives who lived among the streams below Mount St. Helens seasonally visited the mountain's wooded flanks to hunt, fish, pick huckleberries, and collect bear grass for baskets; temporary camps were made during these expeditions. However, probably only youths on spirit quests—those seeking exceptionally powerful guardian spirits—ventured above timberline.

The best-known legend involving the volcano is the story of the Bridge of the Gods and the creation of the Columbia Gorge. In most versions, Mount Hood and Mount Adams, sons of the Great Spirit, fought over a beautiful female mountain. The brothers shook the earth, blocked the sunlight, threw fire at each other, burned the forests, drove off the animals, and covered with ash the plants needed by the people. The fight cracked the Cascade Range, forming a canyon that emptied a huge lake east of the mountains.

The Great Spirit returned and was furious. He left the Bridge of the Gods across the Columbia River as a monument to peace and placed an elderly, weathered female mountain, Loowit, now known as Mount St. Helens, at the bridge as a peacemaker and a reminder to the brothers of how transient youthful beauty is.

Slowly the scars of the battle healed: the green forests returned, and the brothers again wore white coats. But after many years of happiness, jealousy between the brothers again erupted into battle. The earth shook so hard that the Bridge of the Gods was destroyed. Loowit tried to stop the fight, but she was badly battered and fell into the river. As a reward for her bravery, the Great Spirit gave Loowit one wish; she replied that she would like to be young and beautiful again. The Great Spirit granted her wish, but told her that her mind would have to remain old. Loowit replied that she preferred it that way. Since nearly all of her friends had passed away and been replaced by upstarts, she moved off by herself, away from the other mountains. (For a fuller account of this famous legend, see my book *Bridge of the Gods, Mountains of Fire: A Return to the Columbia Gorge*, 1980, distributed by The Mountaineers.)

Falling to Pieces

European exploration of the Pacific Northwest began in earnest near the end of the eighteenth century, when the great abundance of fur-bearing animals, especially sea otters and beavers, attracted trading ships from around the world. British explorer George Vancouver sighted Mount St. Helens in 1792 and gave the peak its present name in honor of British diplomat Alleyne Fitz-herbert, the Lord of St. Helens (a city near Liverpool), who negotiated with John Adams during our revolution.

The next recorded sighting of Mount St. Helens was by the Lewis and Clark Expedition in 1805. Lieutenant William Clark was fascinated by the mountain; he wrote in his journal that it rose "something in the form of a Sugar lofe" and was the "most noble looking object of its kind in nature."

Between the visits of Vancouver and Clark, Mount St. Helens experienced a major eruption, which evidently went unnoticed by the area's fur traders, probably because of the region's notoriously cloudy weather. However, this huge eruption occurring about 1802 spread ash across what later became Idaho and eastern Washington, and the ashfall became part of the oral tradition of the tribes in those areas. Decades later, as documented in the journal *Northwest Discovery* (Vol. 1, No. 1, 1980) and Kenneth Holmes' *Mount St. Helens: Lady with a Past* (Salem Press, 1980), missionaries at the Tshimakain Mission (near Spokane) recorded stories told among the local tribes about the time that ash "fell to the depth of six inches" during "a very long night with heavy thunder." Scientific evidence only recently confirmed this turn-of-the-century eruption.

Kalispel Indians from what is now northern Idaho told physician/explorer George Suckley of the afternoon when "it rained cinders and fire." The tribe "supposed that the sun had burnt up, and that there was an end of all things. The next morning, when the sun arose, they were so delighted as to have a great dance and a feast."

The Sanpoil Indians told ethnologist Verne Ray that they were so scared by the ashfall that "the whole summer was spent in praying." The people even danced—something they seldom did except in winter. The nearby Nespelem Indians told another ethnologist, James Teit, that they were afraid that the ash "prognosticated evil"; they "prayed to the 'dry snow,' called it 'Chief' and 'Mystery' and asked it to explain itself and tell why it came."

A Spokane chief told the United States' 1841 Wilkes Expedition that his people thought that the ash meant that "the world was falling to pieces." The top medicine man assured the tribe that the world was not ending—at least not yet. But he warned them that "soon there will come from the rising sun a different kind of men from any you have yet seen, who will bring with them a book, and will teach you everything, and after that the world will fall to pieces." Other Spokane accounts told of a massive earthquake and the starvation of many people during the harsh winter that followed the ashfall.

By then, the world was already falling apart for the Native Americans near Mount St. Helens; they were devastated by the diseases brought by the white newcomers. Following a turn-of-the-century smallpox epidemic, a wave of malaria or flu around 1830 killed more than 90 percent of the natives living west of the mountain; measles increased the toll. (The more-nomadic tribes east of the Cascade Range, including the Klickitats, were generally less affected.) In 1825 the British built Fort Vancouver at the confluence of the Willamette and Columbia rivers, and it became the regional headquarters for the Hudson's Bay Company empire for two decades, until the U.S. gained control of the region.

The first recorded eyewitness account of a Mount St. Helens eruption was in 1835, when Meredith Gairdner, a physician at Fort Vancouver, saw ashfall during a couple of unusually hazy days. He wrote in a letter that he found "the mountain destitute of its cover of everlasting snow" and saw what "appeared to be lava flows" through his telescope. He wrote that there was a similar period of haze in 1831, which, in retrospect, he thought was also an eruption.

A major cycle of eruptions began in 1842 and coincided with the great migration of pioneers across the Oregon Trail into the depopulated valleys west of the Cascade Range. On November 22, 1842, Reverend Josiah L. Parrish, who was in a meeting at Champoeg, the site of the Methodist mission on the lower Willamette River, stepped outside and noticed that Mount St. Helens was erupting. But, as he later wrote, when he told Jason Lee and the other missionaries still inside, they "laughed the idea to scorn." Finally, the men stepped outside, where they "saw arising from its summit, immense and beautiful scrolls of what seemed to be pure white steam, which rose many degrees into the heavens," while down next to "the mountain's top, the substance was black as ink." The following day, Parrish noticed that "she had changed her snowy dress of pure white for somber black mantle" and that later "flames were seen for a long time issuing from a crater on the south side of the mountain, two-thirds of the way up."

Further eruptions over the next few days dumped ash from the Pacific Ocean eastward at least to The Dalles, where "the winds had wafted its ashes to the door of the missionaries." However, the missionaries arose the next morning to find that "the ejected ashes were falling with a mist-like appearance, covering the leaves, fences, and stone with a light, fine, gritty substance, in appearance like hoar frost, some specimens of which were collected."

These specimens were given to U.S. Army explorer John Fremont the following year, but he later lost them during a flash flood in Kansas on the way back to the East.

Another Methodist missionary, Elijah White, wrote of the mountain that "immense quantities of melted lava were rolling down its sides and inundating the plains below." This account is probably exaggerated, but there were other eyewitness accounts of lava flows during this series of eruptions, as well as some reports of dead fish in the Toutle River.

The major eruptions of this cycle were between 1842 and 1844, but sporadic volcanic activity lasted until 1857. The last known eruption was in April 1857; the *Washington Republican*, a Steilacoom newspaper, noted that the peak had "for the last few days been emitting huge volumes of dense smoke and fire, presenting a grand and sublime spectacle."

In the summer of 1853, Captain George McClellan and his U.S. Army survey expedition cleared a trail that went up the Lewis River and crossed the Cascades south of Mount Adams. They found some villages along the Lewis and a fishing camp above the present town of Yacolt. At this time, there were still Cowlitz Indians living up the Lewis River who had never seen white people. Although there were settlers at Woodland (near the mouth of the Lewis River) and along the Cowlitz River as early as 1845, most pioneers went to the Willamette Valley south of the Columbia River.

Then in 1855 the U.S. government forced most Northwest tribes to sign treaties and established reservations for Indians to clear valuable land for the settlers. The Cowlitz, however, refused to sign a treaty (and are still fighting to get federal recognition of their tribe). By then, even though Mount St. Helens' 123-year period of dormancy had not yet begun, some settlers had already climbed to the summit.

Terra Incognita

The earliest known ascent of Mount St. Helens was in August 1853 by a group of men led by Thomas J. Dryer, the first editor of *The Oregonian*, a Portland newspaper. The two-week trip from Vancouver was made by horseback along the newly cleared Lewis River trail, then by foot up the south slope, which Dryer called "sublimely grand and impossible to describe." Nevertheless, the newspaperman wrote of "blackened piles of lava which were thrown into ridges hundreds of feet high in every imaginable shape of primitive formation." Dryer felt that the mountain was "seeming to lift its head above and struggling to be released from its compressed position," which "impressed the mind of the beholder with the power of compliance and the insignificance of human power when compared to that of Nature's God."

By the year Dryer's party climbed the volcano, the crater on the south side, which was described by witnesses to the 1840s eruptions, had disappeared below snow and the forming glaciers. Dryer did see the crater on the northwest flank and wrote that "smoke was continually issuing from its mouth." In 1854, six months after the ascent, *The Oregonian* updated its coverage, reporting that there was "more smoke issuing from it than there was then, which indicates that the volcanic fires are rapidly increasing within the bowels of this majestic mountain."

In 1860 the second known ascent of Mount St. Helens was made. It is thoroughly described in an amusing 1861 booklet, *Gold Hunting in the Cascade Mountains*, written by one of the explorers under the pseudonym of Loo-wit Lat-kla. The book also relates a tale about an earlier attempt to climb Mount St. Helens: Some employees of the Hudson's Bay Company found, with some trouble, an Indian guide willing to take them to timberline. But

MOUNT ST. HELENS FROM LAVA FIELDS.

This photo of the lava beds on the south slope of Mount St. Helens was taken by the Kiser Brothers, Portland-based photographers, in 1903. They claimed that is was the first photograph taken of the 1900-year-old lava flow.

when the party was part way up the Lewis River, a sudden rainstorm drenched them. Half of the men wanted to return home, and the guide refused to proceed without more blankets. The men who wanted to continue the journey threatened to shoot the native guide, but he was protected by the mutineers. Finally, the disgruntled explorers gave up and returned to civilization, forfeiting what could have been a first ascent.

The August 1860 climb of the volcano was made by a group of six settlers who headed up the Lewis River to hunt elk, prospect for gold, and "rusticate awhile." They followed the Simcoe (Klickitat) Trail up the river past the homesteads at the lush "Cha-la-cha Prairie" (near the present location of the Monument headquarters), but the men soon bored of prospecting in the Lewis River "diggings." Reasoning that the gold hunting would be better further up the side streams, the party found a Klickitat Indian, John Staps, who, with some friends, finally agreed to "pilot" them through the thick undergrowth on Mount St. Helens' steep ridges up to the base of the volcano. After a long, torturous climb, the party found the peak "standing like a hoary-headed giant amongst an army of dwarfs."

At timberline the Indians left the others and headed "toward a beautiful prairie of some three thousand acres, lying on the top of the ridge to the southwest, where mountain sheep, black-tail deer, and woodchuck are numerous." The pioneer party continued on toward the summit, finally reaching it after climbing for hours. The author, unaware of Dryer's climb, declared that "the top of Mount St. Helens ceased to be a *Terra incognita*." The Columbia and Willamette rivers "looked like streaks of silver on a groundwork of velvet," and the vista was "the

These climbers were having lunch at the Lizard during a 1908 ascent of the volcano.

most gorgeous, the most sublimely grand, picturesque, and wonderfully attractive spectacle upon which the eye of man ever feasted." The "yawning crater" seen by Dryer was still visible on the north slope, but it had become as "cold as the snow around it." Spirit Lake looked "like a splendid jewel in an enamelled setting, as it reflected the beautiful, deep-green shadows of the surrounding forest."

The author seemed to find religion atop the volcano: "[We] felt as if nothing was easier than to soar from crag to crag and from peak to peak, but the intense cold served to bring us to reason again and make us feel that we were yet in the *flesh*." During the descent, the party almost slid into a huge crevasse. When steam rose from the crevasse, the author predicted that "we may yet live to witness another eruption of Mount St. Helens."

Back at timberline after sunset, the Indian guides fed the exhausted climbers two deer and a huge woodchuck, but the Indians "predicted a tremendous storm and admonished us to hurry from the mountain before it came upon us, because the Tie [God] was mad and meant to punish us for our invasion of his domain." The party wanted to go on to Spirit Lake, but the leader changed his mind when "the most terrific rain storm I ever witnessed came down upon our pathway, saturating everything." Snow suddenly covered the peak from timberline to the summit. The adventurers hurried home, their trip hindered by floods.

Mount St. Helens remained almost "terra incognita" for decades, although a few more people climbed it before the turn of the century. The crater on the north slope disappeared beneath glaciers sometime between the McBride ascent of 1874 and the 1883 expedition, which included the first women to reach the summit. The first north-side ascent was probably made in 1893 by Colonel Plummer's party; its guide, Leschi, is thought to be the first Indian, at least in recent times, to climb to the top.

Developing The Spirit

The Northern Pacific Railroad was completed from Kalama to Tacoma in 1873, stimulating the development of the region west of Mount St. Helens. Kalama and Centerville (Centralia) boomed in the 1870s, the first store in Woodland opened in 1861, and Kelso was platted in 1884. The town of Toutle was founded in 1876. Logging of the watershed followed a decade later, and a logging railroad was built up the valley in 1895. Yale on the Lewis River was founded in 1867, and the Speelyai mill opened there in 1880. Yacolt became a mill town.

However, development arrived slowly at Mount St. Helens; the peak was away from the navigable waterways, the rugged canyons surrounding it were nearly impassable, and its volcanic origins were not in the ancient past. Robert Lange homesteaded downriver from Spirit Lake in 1879 and built a trading post. Mining began just north of the volcano in 1891—two years after Washington became a state—and the St. Helens Mining District was established in 1892. Under pressure from prospectors, the county build the first wagon road from Castle Rock to Spirit Lake in 1901.

Spirit Lake road, c. 1910
Daniel Stanford
Warnock photo
OREGON HISTORICAL SOCIETY
NEG. ORHI 81643

Many visitors came to Mount St. Helens to hunt elk on the now partially wooded lava fields which had once flowed south into the Lewis River. Ole Peterson, a pioneer who settled east of Cougar, found the first of the lava-tube caves on the volcano's south side while hunting deer in 1895. Ole's Cave soon became a popular tourist attraction—as did Ole, an eccentric hermit. The trail to Ole's Cave has been obliterated, in part to protect its rare species of bats. (Most of the numerous other local lava caves were not found until after World War II.) This photo of Ole's Cave was taken by the Kiser Brothers in 1903.

Dr. Henry Coe bought out Andy Olsen's mining claims and later sold stock to Teddy Roosevelt. Lange traveled to Germany, where he borrowed a quarter-million dollars to develop his claims next to Coe's. Barges were used to haul machinery and ore across Spirit Lake, and a telephone line was installed up to Lange's mine in 1906.

A fire at Lange's mine, started by the smudge pots miners used to keep flies off their horses, burned the south side of Mount Margaret in 1908. The mining fizzled out by 1911, although some gold, silver, copper, and other metals have been taken out over the years. Mining claims continued to be filed, primarily to gain ownership of the valuable timber.

Mount St. Helens was first included in a forest reserve in the 1890s and became part of Columbia National Forest in 1908, during a period of huge forest fires. The U.S. Forest Service built a ranger station at Spirit Lake in 1913. The trail from Spirit Lake to Trout Lake was blazed in the early 1900s, but most of the area's trails were built in the 1930s by the Civilian Conservation Corps (CCC). Four youth camps, beginning with the Portland YMCA camp in 1913, were built at Spirit Lake, as were a few private resorts and many private cabins. Public campgrounds were built at the lake in the 1930s. Coe's dam raised the level of Spirit Lake a couple of feet, and three·large power-generating dams were built on the Lewis River just south of the volcano.

With road access to Spirit Lake and later to a skiing area known as Timberline, climbing Mount St. Helens became a popular pastime in the Pacific Northwest, especially among outdoor clubs. During one weekend in 1938, 2250 people visited Spirit Lake. A new road was finished from Castle Rock to the lake the following year; it was paved in 1946. The paved road to Timberline was finished in 1962 to provide access to a planned downhill ski resort, but avalanches made the project impractical.

During the years of development, the volcano remained *almost* quiet. In 1898 the *Seattle Post-Intelligencer* newspaper reported that "great volumes of smoke emitting from its crater." The local people felt "great consternation" and were "naturally much excited and somewhat alarmed" at first, but the incident was soon forgotten.

Logging near Mount St. Helens c. 1910

Five years later, in 1903, three people caught in a storm near timberline heard a "terrible explosion," followed by a "violent trembling of the earth" and "a hailstorm of rocks and dust." The eruption was "so severe" that the party was "thrown to their knees, rocks were hurled in different directions, and the trees swayed to and fro as if in a hurricane."

Another minor eruption took place in the winter of 1921. Newlyweds Mr. and Mrs. Claude Crum told the *Kelsonian* newspaper that they were in a cabin at Spirit Lake when "it became dark as night in the afternoon, and there was a terrific electric storm." Three days later, they were making the rounds of their trap line and found that the mountain's north and northeast slopes "were dark with a fine powder like cinder dust."

Mount St. Helens then quieted down for a few decades, and people quickly forgot that the beautiful mountain was an active volcano.

New Wilderness

The name of the productive national forest surrounding Mount St. Helens was changed in 1949 to honor the founder of the U.S. Forest Service, Gifford Pinchot, who had died three years earlier. The management of "the GP," as the national forest is usually referred to locally, has been controversial, with conservationists charging that the timber industry has been getting its way most of the time.

In 1949 there were 655 miles of roads in the Gifford Pinchot National Forest; by 1975 there were 2300 miles—and few roadless areas remained for hikers and wildlife. The mileage of trails plummeted; more than half of them were converted to logging roads. The people who once visited Spirit Lake and Mount St. Helens for the solitude and beauty were faced with more clearcuts, motorboats on Spirit Lake, and snowmobiles and other off-road vehicles (ORVs). Most of the fireworks surrounding the volcano in the three decades previous to the 1980 eruptions were between conservationists on one side and logging companies and motorized recreationalists on the other.

The U.S. Forest Service states that "timber harvesting has been quite extensive, primarily on the south and east sides" around Mount St. Helens, but the agency and the timber industry claim that the large cut is needed to provide lumber and jobs—that clearcutting is an economic necessity. The management of the lands around the volcano was complicated by the checkerboard of private lands—primarily owned by Weyerhaeuser, Champion International, Peterson Manufacturing, and Burlington Northern Railroad—within the national forest. Burlington Northern, through nineteenth century government land grants to railroads, even owned the summit of Mount St. Helens until after the 1980 eruption.

Clearcutting moved swiftly up Mount St. Helens' streams, including on lands where the Forest Service later found that the regeneration (regrowth) potential was less than originally estimated. Efforts to replant the timberline clearcuts failed; once the pioneer vegetation was destroyed, the pumice again became a desert in summer.

Only the north side of the mountain — where the blast damage was most severe — remained in a seminatural state by 1980. Fisheries were damaged by dams and erosion from logging and road building, and there were other serious threats, such as the open-pit copper mine planned on the north side by a subsidiary of Pennzoil.

The clearcutting around this lake, which is just outside the Monument boundary near Vanson Peak, was done after the 1980 eruption. While the logging practices are far worse on the private lands west of the Monument, the logging of the national forest east of Mount St. Helens is also very controversial.

When Mount St. Helens erupted in 1980, conservationists were working to protect the mountain within a national monument or scenic area managed by the National Park Service. They weren't getting very far, however. Ironically, shortly before the volcano returned to life, a noted conservationist, pleading for the protection of Washington's "gentler, more vulnerable Southern Cascades," wrote that the North Cascades were largely protected by their ruggedness, but around Mount St. Helens, "nature must depend heavily upon man with a sensitivity toward wild lands to come to her defense."

The spectacular eruption, of course, did help to get significant protection for Mount St. Helens. After the 1980 eruption, the Mount St. Helens Protective Association and other conservationist groups pushed for a 216,000-acre national monument. The Forest Service countered with a proposal for a small 76,000-acre preserve, and—while Congress slowly deliberated—many areas were salvage logged, such as around Ryan Lake, that conservationists wanted included.

Scientists pleaded with Congress to set aside a large preserve to aid crucial research. In 1982, despite the strong opposition of the Reagan administration and the timber industry, Congress finally established the compromise 110,300-acre Mount St. Helens National Volcanic Monument.

A comprehensive management plan has been adopted to guide development of the National Volcanic Monument, and—with the volcano's cooperation—the Forest Service has opened up much of the landscape around the mountain to public use. A new road has been built to Windy Ridge overlooking the heart of the Monument, and trails have been constructed into spectacular portions of the blast zone.

The publicity surrounding the eruption has helped get funds to build recreational facilities at the volcano. The Forest Service does have excellent staff developing visitor facilities, trails, and interpretive programs; and with the large timber cut, the agency has an opportunity to spend more on wildlife, recreation, and interpretation. Public lands near the Monument could become a model of better logging practices.

Some of the landscape around Mount St. Helens, that portion included within the Monument, now has a new start and according to the Act of Congress will be essentially left alone, new wilderness for us to explore and learn from.

3. VISITING THE VOLCANO

Because Mount St. Helens continues to remain relatively calm after its 1980 eruptions, more and more of the landscape around it is being opened to hikers, climbers, backpackers, sightseers, photographers, student groups, and other visitors.

It is possible to get views of Mount St. Helens from near Interstate 5 (I-5), including from the visitor center. However, a day-long trip to the east side of the volcano—especially the Windy Ridge and Spirit Lake viewpoints—is the minimum necessary to begin appreciating what the National Volcanic Monument has to offer.

The Spirit Lake Highway (SR-504), much of which was destroyed by mudflows in 1980, leads from I-5 (near Castle Rock) 5 miles to the Monument's visitor center. The road, formerly the main route for Mount St. Helens visitors, is being rebuilt further up the North Fork Toutle River and will provide close views of the volcano and crater and access to trails only a short (hour-plus) drive from I-5. The planned Coldwater Lake/Johnston Ridge visitor facilities and SR-504 are scheduled to be completed by 1992. For now, however, the most spectacular routes, trails, and views are those on the east side of the volcano.

Since Mount St. Helens is a young and active volcano, it may erupt at any time. When such indicators as increased seismic activity and gas emissions signal possible eruptions, the area around the volcano will be closed to the public. Call ahead to learn the mountain's current status.

Getting to Mount St. Helens

To reach the east side of the volcano from Interstate 5 (I-5), it is generally best to make a loop, reaching Forest Road 25 from the north via Highway US-12, following Forest Road 26 into the Monument, and then taking Forest Road 99 to the Windy Ridge and Spirit Lake viewpoints. To complete the loop back to I-5, descend Road 99 to Road 25, and take Road 25 south to Highway SR-503/Forest Road 90. Portions of these roads are often closed for construction, so contact the U.S. Forest Service for up-to-date information. See *Further Information* in this chapter for addresses and phone numbers.

The northern end of the Monument, reached primarily from Road 26, was the main hiking and backcountry area before the 1980 blast—and will be again. Fascinating trails and viewpoints exist on the west side of the mountain, but access is still difficult. Although it has been ravaged by logging and is the "backside" of the volcano (and thus there are no views of the steaming crater), the south side of Mount St. Helens has many interesting locations, such as Lahar Viewpoint (on a massive mudflow), and great trails, including one inside a lava tube, Ape Cave.

Allow yourself plenty of time as driving times on these curvy roads are much greater than the distances suggest. For example, it takes about two hours (with stops) to reach the Spirit Lake and Windy Ridge viewpoints from Randle, and another three hours or so to get back to I-5 through either Cougar or Randle.

The Forest Service has a Mount St. Helens National Volcanic Monument map-brochure, which complements this guide. Remember, this is a newly designated parkland, so facilities are still being constructed. Delays on roads are still common, and trails are sometimes closed because of blasting.

Windy Ridge

Portions of the Monument, primarily the southern slope, can be visited year-round, but due to snow, the main attractions, such as the Windy Ridge and Spirit Lake viewpoints, are accessible by car only from sometime in June (usually) to late October or early November. The exact dates, however, vary from year to year.

One problem facing visitors, especially hikers, in autumn is that Mount St. Helens is within a national forest, not a national park, and so hunting is allowed in much of the Monument. Especially during elk season, the southern part of the Monument is very popular with hunters, who often use such trails as Goat Marsh Trail 237 and Toutle Trail 238.

Gas is not available within the Monument, so be sure to have a full tank. There is a snack shop on Road 99 across from the Cascade Peaks Viewpoint, but other than that, food is not available. Bear Meadow, Meta Lake, and Windy Ridge interpretive sites have barrier-free facilities, as does Pine Creek Information Station.

Activities

Hiking. Hiking and backpacking around Mount St. Helens are becoming more popular as additional areas are opened to the public. As often as not, hikers and backpackers have to carry water, since the streams that do exist are usually muddy. Backcountry permits are not required, but climbing permits (see below) are needed above 4800 feet (about timberline) for much of the year. The crater is now open to the public when the crater floor is covered with snow; a permit is required, and camping in the crater is not allowed.

Climbing. The south side of Mount St. Helens was reopened to climbing in 1987. Permits (free) are required to climb above timberline from May 16 through October 31. Advance permits (70 per day) are available from Monument headquarters in person or by mail (Mount St. Helens NVM Headquarters, Rt. 1, Box 369, Amboy, WA 98601, 206-247-5800). An additional 30 permits are issued daily, beginning at 11 A.M., at Jack's Restaurant and Store on Highway SR-503 (22 miles east of I-5). The permits are good for 36 hours, so climbers can camp above timberline the night before their ascent. Climbers are required to sign in at Yale Park (west of Cougar) before and after their climbs year-round.

To climb the 8365-foot volcano, it is a good idea to bring sun protection and goggles (ash is troublesome in summer), sturdy boots, windbreakers, gaiters (to keep ash out), and—during much of the year—ice axes, crampons, and rope. The crater rim is very unstable! This is a long, tough climb, so those attempting it should be in good condition. Be sure to bring enough water (or other liquids) and emergency gear in case a storm suddenly appears. See the sections on the two main climbing routes, Ptarmigan Trail 216A and Butte Camp Trail 238A, for more details.

Camping. There are no campgrounds within the small Monument, but good developed campgrounds, public and private, exist near the Monument. Camping outside of developed campgrounds is generally allowed throughout the national forest, but when the fire danger is high, fires are not allowed except in developed campgrounds.

The Forest Service's large Iron Creek Campground south of Randle is in pleasant old-growth forest and provides convenient access to the eastern side of the volcano. Tower Rock and other Forest Service campgrounds are located east of Iron Creek. Campgrounds southeast of the Monument include Lower Falls, a primitive campground (no potable water) along the Lewis River. See the Forest Service's Gifford Pinchot National Forest map for other campgrounds east of Mount St. Helens.

Speelyai Bay, Cougar, Beaver Bay, and Swift campgrounds along Highway SR-503/Road 90 near Cougar are operated by Pacific Power and Light (PP&L), the utility that owns the Lewis River dams. There are motels, private campgrounds, and recreational-vehicle parks along the main access roads—SR-503/Forest Road 90 south of the Monument and Highway US-12 north of it.

Northwest of Mount St. Helens, there are numerous Washington state parks with campgrounds, including Seaquest—across the road from the visitor center—and Lewis and Clark—a mile off US-12 (near Interstate 5). Merrill Lake Campground off Forest Road 81 north of Cougar is operated by the state's Department of Natural Resources and is a favorite with fishermen and hunters. Also along Road 81 are numerous informal camping spots developed over the years by hunting parties.

Cross-country Skiing. Cross-country skiing is popular on the south side of Mount. St. Helens, but so is snowmobiling. Forest Service planners are trying to separate the two groups, but snowmobilers, having had the run of the mountain for years, are resisting restrictions. Progress is being made, and a new ski trail is being built to help separate the two user groups, which presently have to share the closed section of Forest Road 83 to reach many of their respective playgrounds.

The south side of the mountain is popular in winter because the mudflows and numerous clearcuts provide long views and open areas for skiing. The main centers for winter activities are the parking areas on Forest Road 81 (near its junction with Road 83) and Road 83 (at its junction with the side road to Marble Mountain). Sno-Park permits, which are available at stores in Cougar and other nearby towns, are required to park here in winter.

The Forest Service in 1987 completed two cross-country ski trails off Road 83, Sasquatch Loop (236) and June Lake (216B), and is working on two more, Swift Creek (244) and Wapiti (south of Road 83). Pine Creek Trail 216C, which goes to a shelter, is good for cross-country skiing, and Ape Canyon Trail 234 is well suited for winter camping (though, thanks to snowmobiles, solitude is hard to find). The Swift Creek cross-country trail is the main route for winter climbs of the volcano. Road

81 and its trails, such as Toutle (Blue Lake), also provide cross-country skiing opportunities, but the Road 81 Sno-Park is dominated by snowmobilers. (For more information see Klindt Vielbig's *Cross-country Ski Routes of Oregon's Cascades*, The Mountaineers, 1984. This guidebook has a section on additional ski routes on the south side of Mount St. Helens.)

Other Activities. Many of the roads around Mount St. Helens are gravel and thus too rough for most touring bicycles, but are fine for mountain bikes. However, the roads leading to the Monument are heavily used by speeding logging trucks, as well as motorhomes driven by people not used to mountain roads, making bicycle travel quite perilous. The road-guide section notes which roads are paved. Forest Road 99 (to the Windy Ridge and Spirit Lake viewpoints), recently paved and widened to two lanes, is especially good for bicycling. The use of mountain bikes on trails within the blast area is harmful to the trails and thus strongly discouraged.

The reservoirs along the Lewis River south of the volcano are popular with fishermen, campers, motor- and sailboaters, swimmers, and wind surfers. Nearby rivers, such as the Cispus, are popular with rafters.

Although the landscape around Mount St. Helens is no longer as stark and spectacular as it was immediately following the 1980 eruptions, flights over the volcano still offer unequaled views of the altered landscape.

Interpretive talks and walks are conducted during summer at numerous locations, including the visitor center, Windy Ridge, Meta Lake, Cedar Flats, Ape Cave (lantern tours), Norway Pass, Harmony Falls, and Lahar Viewpoint. There are evening campfire programs at Iron Creek, Cougar, and Swift campgrounds. Schedules of talks, walks, and campfire programs are available from the Forest Service.

Further Information

Unless it is way out of your way, pay a visit to the visitor center, northwest of the Monument. The visitor center (barrier-free access) has many excellent exhibits, including a model of the volcano, which helps you orient yourself before going to the Monument. The ten-minute audio-visual presentation has spectacular photography of the 1980 eruptions, and a short trail along Silver Lake provides views of Mount St. Helens.

The visitor center is open from 9 A.M. to 6 P.M. in summer and from 9 A.M. to 5 P.M. in winter. It is open year-round except for Thanksgiving and a few days at Christmas. Phone 206-274-4038 for a recorded message with up-to-date information. (For climbing information, call 206-247-5800.) Natural history books and other educational publications are for sale at the visitor center and the Pine Creek Information Center.

Helpful Forest Service publications include a map-brochure, *Mount St. Helens National Monument* ($1.00), and a free quarterly newspaper, *Volcano Review*. Information can be obtained in person at the visitor center, the headquarters on Highway SR-503 near Amboy south of the Monument, the Randle Ranger Station north of the Monument, and (during summer only) at the Pine Creek Information Station south of the Monument and Woods Creek Information Station 5 miles south of Randle. Also, an information and lantern-rental building is scheduled to open at Ape Cave in 1988.

To get further information before your trip, contact:

Mount St. Helens NVM
  Headquarters
Route 1, Box 369
Amboy, WA 98601
206-247-5473

Mount St. Helens
  Visitor Center
3029 Spirit Lake Highway
Castle Rock, WA 98611
206-274-4038

Nearby Volcanic Areas

Near Mount St. Helens, and especially within the Gifford Pinchot National Forest to the east, there are numerous fascinating examples of volcanism, volcanic activity. Most obvious, of course, are the other large stratovolcanoes, especially Mount Rainier to the north, Mount Adams to the east, and Mount Hood to the south.

Indian Heaven Wilderness, a wonderland of cinder cones and countless lakes and tarns, sits atop a high plateau southwest of Mount Adams. At the southern edge of this wilderness rises Red Mountain, a volcano with a fire lookout atop it. Just south of Indian Heaven lies Big Lava Beds, a 14,000-acre lava flow so recent that only dwarf trees are growing on it. No trails penetrate this lava jumble, but part of the Pacific Crest Trail runs along its western edge. There are also nearby lava tubes.

Southeast of Mount St. Helens, the Columbia Gorge National Scenic Area, where the mighty Columbia River cuts a sea-level passage through the Cascade Range, has many diverse examples of volcanic activity. Dormant volcanoes, such as Larch Mountain (Oregon), line the Gorge's rim. Most of the Gorge's famous waterfalls drop over basalt cliffs. In some places, the lava, which came from what is now northeast Oregon, is up to 2000 feet thick. Lava flows came down both the White Salmon and Hood River valleys; good examples can be seen by rafting down the White Salmon River.

Gifford Pinchot
  National Forest
6926 East Fourth Plain
Vancouver, WA 98668
206-696-7500

Washington State Parks
  & Recreation Commission
7150 Clearwater Lane
Olympia, WA 98505
800-562-0990

Hazards and Etiquette

Hiking in the backcountry entails unavoidable risk that every hiker assumes and must be aware of and respect. The fact that a trail is described in this book is not a representation that it will be safe for you. Trails vary greatly in difficulty and in the degree of conditioning and agility one needs to enjoy them safely. On some hikes routes may have changed or conditions may have deteriorated since the descriptions were written.

You can minimize your risks on the trail by being knowledgeable, prepared, and alert. There is not space in this book for a general treatise on safety in the mountains, but there are a number of good books and public courses on the subject, and you should take advantage of them to increase your knowledge.

These warnings are not intended to scare you off the trails. Hundreds of thousands of people have safe and enjoyable hikes every year. However, one element of the beauty, freedom, and excitement of the wilderness is the presence of risks that do not confront us at home (most of us, anyway). When you hike, you assume those risks. Use your common sense and plan ahead.

Probably the worst danger in the Monument is unstable ground; tephra deposits can be slippery to walk on, and ash landslides are common. There are no poisonous snakes or insects in the Monument; the worst "pests" are mosquitos and yellow jackets. It is no longer safe, of course, to drink water in the backcountry without boiling or otherwise purifying it.

Please be a considerate visitor, both to other visitors and to the natural world—including the year-round residents, the plants and animals that already have enough problems living in the shadow of an active volcano. Pack your litter out, and don't let your pets become pests. Be careful with campfires; no fires are

Meta Lake

allowed in the blast and fringe zones, where there are downed trees. Horses are not allowed in the blast zone, in part to prevent the spread of exotic plant seeds.

Please do not take pumice, pick wildflowers, or otherwise disturb natural and historic features. **Remember, this is an important research area.** (Non-commercial huckleberry and mushroom picking is okay.) Just as you would avoid walking across subalpine meadows, where the damage to wildflowers is obvious, please stay on the trails around the volcano. The plants at Mount St. Helens are often invisible on the barren landscape—but just the same are harmed by being walked on. Tread lightly!

4. ROAD GUIDE

The road system around Mount St. Helens wa built piecemeal and primarily for logging, no tourism. The result is a complex maze that make travel confusing. Unlike Mount Rainier Nationa Park, for example, the Monument has no easy logical road access. To explore the volcano, visitor continually have to leave the Monument an wind through huge clearcuts before returning to another part of the small "park."

Spirit Lake from Forest Road 99

During autumn, many side roads in and near
the Monument, especially on the south side, are
closed to help discourage poaching. The roads
open to the public are marked by posts with green
dots on them. Free road maps are available from
the Forest Service. See **Further Information** in
Chapter 3, Visiting the Volcano, for addresses to
write for information. Call 206-274-4038 for a
recording with up-to-date information.

Highway SR-504

Starting point: Interstate 5 (I-5) at Castle Rock (Exit 49)
Destination: Visitor center and debris dam
Distance: 5 miles to visitor center
Surface: Pavement
Travel season: Year-round
Highlights: Visitor center

State Route 504, the old Spirit Lake Highway, was once the main route to Mount St. Helens and may, when extended, again become the most popular. The old highway's scenic location along the Toutle River was its downfall: The highway was destroyed during the 1980 eruption by Toutle mudflows and floods. The state plans to have the highway rebuilt to near Coldwater Lake in 1991, and Johnston Ridge will become a major viewpoint and visitor attraction. Trails will lead to Windy Ridge.

The visitor center is located along SR-504 at Silver Lake 5 miles east of I-5 and, weather permitting, provides views of the volcano. The new visitor center has excellent exhibits, movies and audio-visual presentations, and interesting wood carvings. Appropriately enough, Silver Lake was formed by mudflows from Mount St. Helens about 3000 years ago.

The May 18, 1980, eruption sent a debris avalanche containing 3.8 billion cubic yards of debris roaring down the North Fork Toutle River. The "toe" of the debris-avalanche deposit reached 14 miles downriver from the volcano (17 miles up the road from the new visitor center), and the deposits sometimes exceeded 500 feet in height. Downstream of the debris-avalanche deposit, extensive flooding wiped out roads and homes, and ash washed down to the Columbia, blocking navigation. Ash deposits in the Toutle and Cowlitz rivers reduced the capacity of these streams, making more flooding likely.

This threat to downriver communities led Congress to authorize the Sediment Retention Structure, better known as the debris dam, which the U.S. Army Corps of Engineers is constructing on the North Fork Toutle River to trap ash being washed down the river (and into the Columbia, a major waterway for commerce). The earth and concrete dam is going to be 184 feet tall and is expected to fill with ash in 45 years. Construction of the debris dam is expected to be completed in late 1989. A previous debris dam (N1) built after the 1980 blast was soon wiped out by a mudflow.

The Corps of Engineers is trying to "contain" nature with other projects, too. The Toutle River debris avalanche created new lakes that could cause flooding if the natural dams that produced them collapse. For example, part of the Toutle mudflow poured into a side tributary, Coldwater Creek, and solidified, forming a dam that created huge Coldwater Lake. To help prevent these natural dams from suddenly breaking, the Corps built artificial outlets at both Coldwater and Castle lakes and a huge tunnel for lowering the level of Spirit Lake. The 8500-foot-long tunnel, which was completed in 1985, drains water from Spirit Lake into Coldwater Creek so that the lake doesn't spill over and cause flooding.

Before construction of the debris dam began, SR-504 had been rebuilt to the toe of the debris-avalanche deposit, and a short trail led to a good viewpoint. Because of the massive construction project, however, this viewpoint and the roads leading to the Vanson Peak trails are no longer accessible. At the present end of SR-504, 17 miles east of the visitor center, a 300-foot-long trail leads to a view of the debris dam. Unless you like to watch huge earth-moving operations, the drive up SR-504 is not especially interesting, although there are good views of the ash-laden Toutle River (as well as numerous souvenir stands) along the way.

Highway SR-503/Forest Road 90

Starting point: Interstate 5 (I-5) at Woodland (Exit 21)
Destination: Road 25 near Pine Creek
Distance: 48 miles
Surface: Pavement
Travel season: Open most of the year
Highlights: Views of Mount St. Helens and mudflows

South of Mount St. Helens, State Route 503 follows the Lewis River from Woodland (30 miles north of Portland) toward Cougar. Along the way, it becomes Forest Road 90, which continues along the Lewis River across the Gifford Pinchot National Forest toward Mount Adams (and other interesting volcanic sites). From Road 90 near the Pine Creek Information Station at the east end of Swift Reservoir, Forest Road 25 heads northward along the east side of the volcano and provides access to the Windy Ridge and Spirit Lake viewpoints.

At Ariel, 11 miles east of I-5, is the Lelooska interpretive center. At Speelyai Hill, 22 miles from I-5, SR-503 turns right (south) and leads a mile up the hill to a good viewpoint of the volcano and then on to Monument headquarters (4 miles before Amboy). Continue straight on what is known as the Lewis River Road (and near Cougar becomes Road 90) to go to Mount St. Helens.

At Yale Park 27 miles from I-5, there are restrooms, water, a beach, a boat ramp, picnic tables, and a "self-service" Forest Service information station, where climbers register before and after scaling Mount St. Helens.

A mile beyond Yale Park, Forest Road 81 heads north to the southwestern side of the volcano. Cougar, a small town with food and gas, is another mile further on Road 90. Eight miles further, shortly after a viewpoint of the south side of the volcano, Forest Road 83 heads north to Ape Cave, Lahar Viewpoint, and trailheads.

After the Road 83 junction, Road 90 continues along the north bank of Swift Reservoir to the Forest Service's Pine Creek Information Station (closed during winter). Most of the Lewis River west of Pine Creek is dammed, and Pacific Power & Light (PP&L), the utility that owns the hydroelectric dams, operates numerous campgrounds and other recreational sites along Road 90.

Just past the Pine Creek Information Station, the road forks. Road 25, straight ahead, leads north to Mount St. Helens and Randle. Road 90 turns sharply to the right and continues eastward, leading to Mount Adams and (via Forest Road 30 through Carson) the Columbia Gorge. Gas, food, equipment rentals, and other services are available at Eagle Cliffs a mile down Road 90 (the last chance before the Monument); and beginning about 5 miles east of the Road 25 junction, numerous hikes from Road 90 lead to scenic waterfalls along the Lewis River.

Highway US-12

Starting point: Interstate 5 (I-5) Exit 68
Destination: Forest Road 25 at Randle
Distance: 49 miles
Surface: Pavement
Travel season: Year-round
Highlights: Year-round view of Mount St. Helens crater

Highway US-12 heads east along the Cowlitz River from I-5 to Morton (32 miles) and Randle (another 17 miles). About 17 miles from I-5, between the towns of Mossyrock and Morton, a short side road—aptly though not imaginatively called Short Road—leads 1.2 miles to an appetizer, a distant view of the crater and lava dome directly to the south. At Randle, gas, food, and most services are available. A Forest Service ranger station is a mile east of town.

Forest Road 25

Starting point: Forest Road 90 junction near Pine Creek
Destination: Forest Road 23 and US-12 at Randle
Distance: 35 miles one way
Surface: Narrow pavement
Travel season: May through November
Highlights: Good views of east side of Mount St. Helens
Trailheads: Crosses Boundary Trail No. 1

Less than a mile from its beginning at Road 90, Forest Road 25 crosses Pine Creek. On the south bank is a large boulder washed downstream by a 1980 mudflow; an interpretive sign provides background information.

A couple of miles further north, at the junction with Forest Road 2588 (a washboard road to the Lahar Viewpoint), Road 25 enters Cedar Flats Research Natural Area, a small but protected old-growth forest on an old mudflow. The trailhead for an easy, 1-mile loop walk (Cedar Flats Trail 320) through tall Douglas fir and western red cedar trees is about a mile further north.

A mile after exiting the research area, Road 25 crosses the aptly named Muddy River. Just past the bridge, interpretive signs explain the formation of the mudflow. Boulders weighing tons were swept miles down the stream by the 1980 mudflows. Both the Pine Creek and Muddy River mudflows make for good cross-country hikes and ski trips.

At Muddy River, Road 25 climbs steeply up a ridge and along a green (but ash-dusted) ridge for 20 miles to the turnoff for Forest Road 99, the main route to Bear Meadow and the Spirit Lake and Windy Ridge viewpoints. Between the Muddy River and Road 99 are some good vistas of the east side of the volcano, and there are interpretive signs at Clearwater Viewpoint (16 miles north of Road 90).

Two miles north of the Road 99 junction is the Forest Road 2516 junction. This steep, dead-end gravel road leads to the Strawberry Mountain trailhead and views of the crater.

Iron Creek Campground, a developed Forest Service site in old-growth woodlands by the Cispus River, is located along Road 25 about 8 miles north of the Road 2516 junction. A mile past the campground is the junction with Forest Road 26, which leads to Ryan Lake and the Spirit Lake and Windy Ridge viewpoints. Randle and Highway US-12, which leads back to Interstate 5, are another 9 miles.

Forest Road 2516

Starting point: Forest Road 25
Destination: Mount St. Helens viewpoint
Distance: 8 miles (dead end)
Surface: Steep gravel (no trailers)
Travel season: July through October
Highlights: Good view of crater and lava dome
Trailheads: Strawberry Mountain

Forest Road 2516, which heads west off Road 25 about 2 miles north of the junction with Forest Road 99, leads to Strawberry Mountain and good roadside views of the lava dome. However, this steep and narrow gravel road is not recommended for trailers or large vehicles.

At 6.5 miles, this road goes through a saddle and into the Ryan Lake/Green River basin. In another mile, Mount St. Helens is visible; continue on for a turnaround.

Strawberry Mountain Trail 220 crosses Forest Road 2516 at the ridgetop, from where it is a mile-long hike up to the top of Strawberry Mountain, the planned site of a fire lookout. (See the trail-guide section.)

Forest Road 26

Starting Point: Forest Road 25, 10 miles south of Randle
Destination: Forest Road 99 near Meta Lake
Distance: 17 miles
Surface: Narrow pavement
Travel season: June through October, sometimes open to
Ryan Lake in winter
Highlights: Ryan Lake, great vistas of blast area
Trailheads: Strawberry Mountain, Goat Mountain (side
road), Green River (side road), Boundary Trail No. 1
(including Norway Pass)

To reach Forest Road 26, go south on Forest Road 23/25 at
Randle. After a mile, the road splits, with the left fork (Road
23) leading to Mount Adams and Trout Lake. The right fork
(Road 25) leads to Woods Creek Information Station (open
summer only) and Mount St. Helens.

Ten miles from Randle, Road 26 heads west off Road 25.
(To reach Iron Creek Campground, continue south on Road
25 for 1 mile.) Road 26 is paved and smooth but narrow, so
bicycling it is fun — but adventuresome. Road 26 is usually
two-way, but is presently sometimes one-way because of
the Forest Road 99 construction.

The first few miles of Road 26 wind through lush vegetation, primarily second-growth forest with many maples
and other deciduous trees that put on dazzling displays of
yellows and reds in October and November. At 3.5 miles
from the Road 25 junction, a side road (045) leads up to the
northern (and least practical) trailhead for Strawberry
Mountain Trail 220.

Eight miles from the Road 25 junction, a side road to the
right (Forest Road 2808) leads a mile to Quartz Creek Big
Trees Trail, which winds through a small grove. The trail is
quite short and can be hiked in 10 to 20 minutes. It is a good
place to get a feel for the evergreen forests that once domi-

grove. The trail is quite short and can be hiked in 10 to 20 minutes. It is a good place to get a feel for the evergreen forests that once dominated this landscape before you enter the blast zone another mile up Road 26. Some of the trees killed by the blast have been left standing in the Quartz Creek valley, primarily at high elevations on the surrounding slopes, but in the area north of Ryan Lake, which Congress left out of the Monument, most were salvage-logged and the area replanted following the 1980 eruptions.

Twelve miles up Road 26, a dirt logging road (Forest Road 2612) leads to the trailheads for the Goat Mountain and Green River trails. Continue 0.2 mile up Road 26 to reach the turnoff to Ryan Lake picnic area, which has toilets. From the parking lot, a 0.6-mile loop trail winds up to the knoll overlooking Ryan Lake, which was heavily impacted by the 1980 blast. Logging slash, blast slash, and helicopter landing pads remain as reminders of the salvage logging. This trail provides good views of the Green River valley (to the west) and Strawberry Mountain (to the east).

From Ryan Lake, Road 26 winds steeply up over a divide, then enters the Monument and snakes through a surreal landscape of downed trees to the Norway Pass (Boundary Trail No. 1) trailhead (16 miles from Road 25). Boundary Trail No. 1 west of the road leads to Norway Pass and Mount Margaret; this is one of the finest trails in the Monument, providing vistas of the crater reflecting in Spirit Lake. Boundary Trail No. 1 east of Road 26 leads to Ghost Lake and Bear Meadow, then continues on toward Mount Adams. This trailhead has barrier-free toilets and potable water.

A mile past the Norway Pass trailhead, Road 26 ends at Road 99. Road 99 to the left (east) descends back to Road 25. Road 99 to the right leads to incredible views of Spirit Lake and the heart of the Monument.

Forest Road 99

Starting point: Forest Road 25
Destination: Windy Ridge and Spirit Lake viewpoints
Distance: 17 miles one way
Surface: Pavement
Travel season: June through October (varies)
Highlights: Meta Lake and spectacular views of Mount
  St. Helens, Spirit Lake, and the blast zone
Trailheads: Boundary Trail No. 1, Independence Pass,
  Harmony, Abraham

From Forest Road 25, Forest Road 99 climbs through green forest and, after Bear Meadow, enters the blast zone. At Bear Meadow are barrier-free toilets, picnic tables, Boundary Trail No. 1 trailheads, and interpretive signs about the famous series of eruption photos taken here on May 18, 1980. Road 99 intersects Road 26 about 9 miles from Road 25; turn right on Road 26 to reach the Norway Pass trailhead (1 mile).

Along Forest Road 99 immediately past the junction with Road 26 is the "miner's car," a large vehicle thrown around by the 1980 blast. A short distance further is the trailhead for a short, paved interpretive trail (barrier-free) to Meta Lake, an enchanting place. The tall trees surrounding the lake were killed by the blast, but thanks to a ridge and the deep snowpack, the smaller trees survived. Fish and other life survived in the ice-covered lake, and the lakeshore now sometimes teems with frogs. Water is available from a pump at the trailhead.

From Meta Lake, Road 99 climbs uphill a mile to Cascade Peaks Viewpoint, which provides exceptional vistas of Mount St. Helens and other Cascade Range volcanoes. A snack bar and toilets are located across the road from the viewpoint. The road that forks off to the left here (Forest Road 2560) returns to Road 25 through

Mount Adams from Windy Ridge

the replanted Clearwater valley. The Forest Service sometimes has Road 2560 closed to public use, but the agency leads interpretive auto tours on weekends.

The fork to the right is the continuation of Road 99 and leads 7 miles—7 unbelievable miles!—to the Spirit Lake viewpoints and the dead end at Windy Ridge Viewpoint. Now that this road has been widened and paved, sightseeing by bicycle is even better. There are numerous turnouts along Road 99, most with extraordinary views of remodeled Spirit Lake.

The Independence Pass trailhead is on the right 1.4 miles from Cascade Peaks Viewpoint. The Harmony trailhead is another 2 miles up Road 99, and this mile-long trail drops down to the shoreline of Spirit Lake. Road 99 ends at Windy Ridge Viewpoint 8 miles from the Road 26 junction. At Windy Ridge are the Plains of Abraham trailhead, a short but near-vertical trail (361 steps) to the top of the ridge, toilets, interpretive signs and, of course, tremendous views in all directions.

Forest Road 83

Starting point: Forest Road 90 near Cougar
Destination: Ape Cave turnoff and Lahar Viewpoint
Distance: 11 miles to Lahar
Surface: First 3 miles paved, rest gravel
Travel season: Open year-round to the Sno-Park at the
    Marble Mountain turnoff
Highlights: Trail of Two Forests, Lahar Viewpoint,
    Pine Creek mudflow
Trailheads: Ape Cave (side road), June Lake, Pine
    Creek, Ape Canyon, cross-country ski trails

Forest Road 83 begins at Road 90 (just beyond Swift
Viewpoint) 8 miles east of Cougar and is the main route
to Ape Cave, Lahar Viewpoint, great trails, and parking
for winter recreation. The first 3 miles of the road (up a
1900-year-old basalt flow) are paved; the rest (over old
mudflows) is well-graded gravel. (This section will be
under construction for part of 1988.)

On the left off Road 83 less than 2 miles north of Road
90, Forest Road 8303 leads to Lava Cast picnic area (0.2
mile) and Ape Cave (1 mile). At Lava Cast, in addition
to vault toilets, there is the marvelous, barrier-free
Trail of Two Forests, a 0.3-mile-long loop on a boardwalk
through two forests: one cast in stone by a lava flow
almost 2000 years ago, the other young trees that have
grown up here since then. Hikers can crawl through a tree
mold, which is especially popular with children—so be
prepared (flashlights and old clothes). The basalt here
is from a fluid lava flow similar to that associated with
Hawaiian-type shield volcanoes rather than stratovolcanoes like Mount St. Helens. (Please protect the moss
and other features by staying on the trail.) See the trail-
guide section for more information on visiting Ape Cave,
one of the longest lava tubes in the world.

A mile north of the Ape Cave turnoff, the pavement ends and Forest Road 81 (see next section) comes in from the left. A Sno-Park winter parking area is a short distance up Road 81, as is the side road (Forest Road 830) to the trailhead for Ptarmigan Trail 216A.

Road 83 to the right continues on 8 miles to the Lahar Viewpoint, an interpretive site on a mudflow. A side road about half way to the Lahar Viewpoint (Forest Road 8312) leads 5 miles to the top of 4116-foot Marble Mountain, a dormant shield volcano that provides excellent views of Mount St. Helens (unfortunately, virtually all the trees between Marble Mountain and timberline on Mount St. Helens have been logged off).

The Monument's main Sno-Park winter parking area is by the Marble Mountain junction. The ski trail up Swift Creek is just past the Sno-Park; the June Lake Trail (for hiking and skiing) is a mile further; and the Sasquatch ski loops are located less than a mile further east.

A mile after Road 83 crosses Pine Creek, where a 1980 lahar (mudflow) swept away the bridge (which has never been found), the road forks. The left branch leads 0.1 mile to Lahar Viewpoint (no facilities).

At the Lahar Viewpoint, a short (650 feet) trail leads to an interpretive site, where visitors can observe how the lahar—caused by the rapid melting of Shoestring Glacier—split into two drainages, which merge again before entering Swift Reservoir. When the snowpack and Shoestring Glacier, which filled the now-visible notch on the east side of the volcano (4.5 miles away), were melted by hot ash and gases on May 18, 1980, the water mixed with rock and ash and moved down the drainage like wet cement, leaving thick deposits. A small part of Shoestring Glacier remains on the volcano. Before 1980, it extended down to 4800 feet elevation and was the lowest glacier on the mountain.

The mudflow can be further explored by walking down the closed road to two streams, one clear and the other usually muddy. The cliff past the second stream shows 13,000 years of stratigraphic bands, layers deposited by earlier mudflows and pyroclastic flows. Downstream is Lava Canyon, where the mudflow scoured the canyon and exposed a previous lava flow, creating waterfalls in the process. The road is going to be extended to the other side of the lahar, where a picnic area and the Lava Canyon trailhead are planned. (The first part of this spectacular trail will be on a barrier-free boardwalk.) Most of the south side of Mount St. Helens has been formed by lahars, so the majority of the drive to Lahar Viewpoint is across lahars old enough to be covered with forests.

Just before the Lahar Viewpoint, Road 83 heads on eastward. In less than a mile, the road forks. The left fork is the continuation of Road 83 and drops into a deep valley, where it dead-ends in 4.4 miles at the future trailhead for Smith Creek Trail 225 (under construction). The right fork is Forest Road 2588, a 7-mile-long washboard shortcut down to Road 25 at Cedar Flats. Through breaks in the trees, this road provides interesting views of "badlands" (pyroclastic deposits) along Pine Creek.

Forest Road 81

Starting point: Forest Road 90 (SR-503) west of Cougar
Destination: Forest Roads 8123 and 83
Distance: 17 miles
Surface: First half paved, rest good gravel (washouts near end sometimes block car passage)
Travel season: May through November
Highlights: Good views along edge of lava flow
Trailheads: Toutle/Butte Camp, Ptarmigan (side road)

Forest Road 81 is a side road that provides access to the southwest part of the Monument; the first part is paved, the rest is gravel. However, a section of Road 81 (about 2 miles before its junction with Forest 83) is often washed out and impassable to cars.

Road 81 begins near a weigh station on SR-503/Road 90 (just over a mile east of Yale Park) and passes below huge clearcuts on near-vertical slopes. At 5 miles, Road 81 passes Merrill Lake, where there is a state Department of Natural Resources (DNR) campground popular with fly fishermen and hunters.

Just past Merrill Lake, Goat Mountain is visible, and 4 miles past the campground, Road 81 turns sharply to the right to go around the monolith. The left fork (straight ahead) is Forest Road 8117, which winds north toward the South Fork Toutle River through clearcuts populated with elk and huckleberries.

After the fork, Road 81 enters the Monument and the pavement ends. There are numerous undeveloped camping sites along Road 81 that have been established over the years by hunting parties. Vine maples line the road here, making it especially scenic in autumn.

There is another fork in the road 3 miles from the first fork; again the right fork is the continuation of Road 81. The left fork (straight ahead) is Forest Road 8123, a gravel road that leads to the Goat Marsh, Toutle (Blue Lake), and Sheep Canyon trailheads.

After the Road 8123 junction, Road 81 heads east across some striking examples of vulcanism. On the left in a mile, among moss-draped snags, is Kalama Springs, the headwaters of the Kalama River. There was a campground here, but a mudflow swept through it in 1980. Far below the road on the south side is scenic McBride Lake.

A mile further, Road 81 passes a lush meadow on the left. The cliff above the meadow is the toe of an old lava flow that came down Mount St. Helens. The road climbs to the top of the lava flow, where the Butte Camp trailhead is located, and then crosses recent ash and rock deposits that have choked many trees.

About 14 miles from Highway SR-503/Road 90, Road 81 crosses mudflows where erosion often makes passage for passenger cars impossible. Just past these mudflows, Forest Road 830 to the north provides access to Ptarmigan Trail 216A, the main climbing route. (Road 830 will be under construction in 1988, so there may be delays.) The last couple of miles of Road 81 are downhill through second-growth forest to Road 83 near Ape Cave.

Forest Road 8123

Starting point: Forest Road 81
Destination: Sheep Canyon and South Fork Toutle River
Distance: 7 miles to Sheep Canyon trailhead
Travel season: June through October
Highlights: Views of Goat Marsh wetlands and South
  Fork Toutle River mudflows (above)
Trailheads: Goat Marsh, Toutle, Sheep Canyon

From Road 81, it is 0.6 mile to the trailhead for easy Goat Marsh Trail 237. Two miles from Road 81, just after a left turn where the old road was washed out, is the new trailhead for hiking to Blue Lake (Toutle Trail 238).

Road 8123 continues for another 5 miles, providing good views of Goat Marsh, a research natural area and the most important wetlands in the Monument. Six miles from Road 81, as the road nears the South Fork Toutle River valley (the logging-caused erosion you see is on timber-company lands), it turns sharply to the right and heads uphill for a mile to a viewpoint and the Sheep Canyon trailhead. Until it is rebuilt, however, this last section of the road is too rough for most cars. (See Sheep Canyon Trail 240 for more information.)

5. TRAIL GUIDE

Compared to most Northwest hiking, hiking around Mount St. Helens can be very hot because of the lack of shade on the mudflows and other open terrain. More often than not, hiking around the volcano is also a dirty business. Especially if conditions are windy, hikers are soon covered with layers of ash—true grit. These inconveniences are minor, however, compared to the exciting opportunities to explore recently created volcanic landscapes unlike any others in this country.

The Forest Service trail planners rated the trails as easy, more difficult, and most difficult. Then they designed the trails accordingly, determining width, maximum steepness, and other standards based on their difficulty ratings. The trails in the northern extremity of the Monument have been designed for horse and hiker use. Two barrier-free trails, Meta Lake and Trail of Two Forests (Lava Cast), have been completed, and a spectacular one is going to be built down Lava Canyon to a series of waterfalls (opposite page).

Many trails are under construction and may be closed because of blasting. Check with the Forest Service for current information. (See Further Information in Chapter 3, Visiting the Volcano, for addresses and phone numbers.)

Loowit Trail 216, scheduled to be completed in the early 1990s, will encircle the volcano and be one of the finest trails anywhere. Feeder trails now lead to finished sections of this trail. The stretch in front of the crater will be the last to be completed.

FACE TO FACE WITH THE VOLCANO
(WINDY RIDGE and SPIRIT LAKE)

The trails northeast of Mount St. Helens are presently the most amazing ones in the Monument, providing vistas of the dome growing in the crater—often reflected in Spirit Lake. These pathways provide a remarkable cross section of the blast zone, with trails through the basin hardest hit by the blast connecting with trails that wind in and out of the edge of the blast zone.

Windy Ridge extends northeast from the east lobe of the crater rim and forms the steep east bank of Spirit Lake. The trailheads for three of the best hikes, those closest to the open side of the crater, are along Forest Road 99, which runs along Windy Ridge. One of these trails, Harmony, provides the only access to Spirit Lake; and a trail now under construction, Smith Creek, will drop off the other side of the ridge and follow Smith Creek downstream to the Muddy River and Lava Canyon.

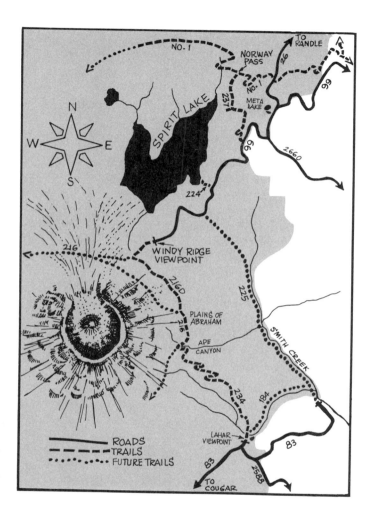

Abraham Trail 216D

Distance: 3.9 miles one way to Loowit Trail 216
Hiking time: Full day for round trip to Plains of
  Abraham
Difficulty: More difficult
Best time to hike: July through October
Trailhead: Forest Road 99

The first half of Abraham Trail 216D, the easiest route to the Plains of Abraham, is the extension of Road 99, which is closed to nonofficial motorized traffic at Windy Ridge Viewpoint. Being a dirt roadbed, this trail is easy to walk. Unlike around the Ryan Lake area, for example, here the jumble of downed trees is covered with deep ash, making the landscape primarily smooth, almost-glazed gray ash. As one returns to the side of the ridge facing the crater, the desertlike terrain is covered with deep tephra (materials blown out of the volcano) and volcanic rocks of all sizes and many colors. (Remember, don't disturb the recovery process by taking souvenir rocks home. Rocks provide shade for budding plants and habitat for small critters.)

Lava dome in 1981

After 1.7 miles, just past a spring, the trail cuts off the road and heads—steeply—up a ridge toward the Plains of Abraham. The road slowly drops into the basin in front of the crater and across what appears to be a desert alluvial fan misplaced in the Pacific Northwest. This road leads down to the vicinity of a future section of the 'round-the-mountain Loowit Trail, which will cross in front of the crater. For now, however, the lake side of the ridge is closed to the public because of dangers and to protect fragile natural features.

Until the area in front of the crater is opened to hikers, the trail to the Plains of Abraham is a great alternative. The trail climbs steeply up a narrow ridge, then drops into the barren (except in July, when wild-flowers are in bloom) "plains." At 3.9 miles from the trailhead, Trail 216A ends at the Plains of Abraham section of Loowit Trail 216, which can be followed to Ape Canyon and on to the Lahar Viewpoint (9 miles from Windy Ridge Viewpoint). For more on these wonderful, Death Valley-like "badlands," see the description of Ape Canyon Trail 234.

Harmony Trail 224

Distance: 1 mile one way
Hiking time: 2 hours for round trip
Difficulty: More difficult
Best time to hike: July through October
Trailhead: Forest Road 99

Spirit Lake was once the primary destination for visitors to Mount St. Helens. Now the only access to the remodeled lake is this short but spectacular trail. It takes about half an hour to hike down to the lake, slightly longer to return to the trailhead. Lacking shade, this trail can be hot; bring water.

Harmony Falls

This trail begins at Harmony Viewpoint on Road 99 (3.7 miles before the road ends at Windy Ridge Viewpoint) and drops down to the shoreline of Spirit Lake. The once lush scene where Harmony Falls cascaded into the lake has been replaced by a barren ledge above a log-strewn beach. The Harmony Lodge site is now under more than a hundred feet of water.

This is a excellent morning hike: the lake is more apt to be calm then—providing

good reflections of the crater—and the upper part of the trail is in shade. This first part of the trail is along a cliff covered with springs and plants associated with dampness, such as ferns. The upper trail is cut through downed trees, but it later emerges onto a barren, almost-flat plain. Only a few lupines now grow on the valley floor, but—if given enough time by the volcano and visitors—a new forest will return here in coming years. Harmony Creek is now usually running clear, but only a small waterfall remains.

The lakeshore, like an ocean beach, is covered with driftwood logs, which make good seats to avoid the ash that covers everything else. (It is very dangerous, however, to swim around or climb on the floating logs, which sometimes blow across the lake at amazing speeds.) The shoreline here is a couple of hundred feet above the pre-1980 shoreline, since the debris avalanche raised the natural dam that forms Spirit Lake, greatly enlarging the lake. Because of all the debris, however, part of the lake is shallower. Slowly, the color of Spirit Lake is returning to the deep blues for which it was once famous.

Independence Pass Trail 227

Distance: 1.3 miles to viewpoint, 2 more to Norway Pass
Hiking time: 2 to 3 hours for round trip to viewpoint
Difficulty: More difficult
Best time to hike: July through October
Trailhead: Forest Road 99

The first 0.3 mile of this scenic trail climbs steeply up to the top of the ridge above the road, a short walk that is rewarded with benches and a map showing key landmarks and how they were changed by the 1980 eruptions. This part of the trail was one of the first rebuilt after the 1980 eruptions, but the dome was so small at first that it was not visible from this point until an eruption in September 1982. The dome since then has grown more than a hundredfold and may someday—unless blown away by more blasts—fill the crater and again form a conical peak (in about 200 years at the present rate of growth).

Harmony Falls Resort, Spirit Lake, Wn.

The trail continues up the ridge and makes a big sweep toward the lake, with continuous views of the steaming crater, as well as the Harmony Creek basin and Spirit Lake below the trail. The trail is cut through the jumble of bare, fallen trees. From this first viewpoint, it is a mile to short side trail leading to a superb viewpoint above Spirit Lake.

Note that the cliffs around Spirit Lake have been scoured clean for more than 200 feet above the water. The debris avalanche sliding into the lake created a huge wave that sloshed up the surrounding shoreline, sweeping it clean of vegetation and leaving much of the forest floating in Spirit Lake.

From the knoll above Spirit Lake, the trail continues another 2 miles north to Norway Pass, where it ends at Boundary Trail No. 1. This section passes below high cliffs and by large basalt monoliths, including 100-foot-high Tephra Pinnacle, rising out of the ash slopes. These formations were hidden by trees before the 1980 eruption. When this part of the trail was being located, a volleyball and a propane tank were found in the ash, probably thrown up from Spirit Lake.

Norway Pass Trail
(Part of Boundary Trail No. 1)

Distance: 2.2 miles to Norway Pass, 9.8 miles to Coldwater Peak
Hiking time: Half-day for round trip to Norway Pass
Difficulty: More difficult
Best time to hike: July through October
Trailhead: Forest Road 26

One of the most spectacular trails in the Monument—if not *the* most spectacular—Boundary Trail No. 1 to 4508-foot-elevation Norway Pass (below and cover) provides exceptional views of the crater and dome with Spirit Lake in the foreground. It is 2.2 miles to the pass, with an elevation gain of a thousand feet, and there are good views of Mount Rainier and other volcanoes.

The trail at one point dips into a sheltered drainage and through a garden of avalanche lilies that survived the 1980 eruption. These beautiful subalpine flowers are common on the slopes of older and long-dormant Cascade volcanoes, such as Mount Rainier, but are still rare at young Mount St. Helens, where soil is still forming and old soil is being exposed by erosion.

Spirit Lake from Mount Margaret backcountry
Wayne Parsons photo, 1976

At Norway Pass is the junction with the Independence Pass Trail, which makes a nice side trip. Past Norway Pass, Boundary Trail No. 1 has been extended into the Mount Margaret backcountry, the main backpacking area before 1980. The trail climbs gently but steadily to a series of points with sweeping vistas. A 0.2-mile-long side trail goes to Mount Margaret. Before Harry's Ridge, a side trail goes south 0.7 mile to the top of Coldwater Peak (about 10 miles from the trailhead). Mountain goats and other wildlife were common here before the 1980 eruption.

Part of this trail past Norway Pass is still under construction, so it may be closed for blasting. When completed, this trail will end at the observatory planned for Johnston Ridge when the reconstruction of Highway SR-504 is done (probably by 1992).

Water is available from a pump at the trailhead. See the section on Boundary Trail No. 1 for information on the portion of this trail east of Road 26.

BIG TREES, LIVE AND DEAD
(NORTHERN END OF MONUMENT)

The northern end of Mount St. Helens National Volcanic Monument was included to protect old-growth forest along the Green River. Shielded by mountains, about two-thirds of the eight miles of old growth that had survived the chainsaw also survived the 1980 eruption. This lush valley is enclosed by 5000-foot peaks, which have connecting trails. The first half of the trail up Goat Mountain follows the edge of the blast zone, but most of this trail system is outside the blast zone and thus provides alternatives to the dusty ones within the most impacted areas. These trails have considerable horseback use (especially during hunting season).

Access to the big trees along the Green River is still difficult. There are two main sets of trailheads: from Forest Road 2612, which heads west from Road 26 at Ryan Lake, and from timber-company roads that wind out of Morton. The eastern end of the Green River Trail is easier to get to, but the first part of the trail is still buried beneath blowdown and logging slash and thus requires a tortuous climb over and along huge logs. To reach the trail from the western end is not much of an alternative: the maze of gravel roads leading to the trailhead can be confusing, an access road has washed out, and the trail drops steeply into the valley of old-growth Douglas firs, requiring a strenuous climb out.

To reach the western ends of the Green River, Vanson Peak, and Goat Mountain trails requires a long drive on gravel logging roads. The maze of private logging roads on this ridge between the Cowlitz and North Fork Toutle rivers looks as if someone threw spaghetti onto a map, and markings are minimal. These roads are sometimes closed by the timber companies because of high fire dangers, and speeding logging trucks are a problem.

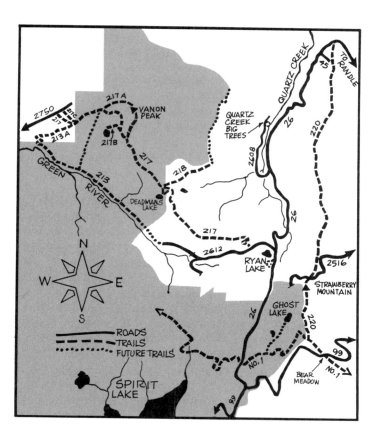

East of Goat Mountain, across Quartz Creek, is a tall ridge capped with 5464-foot Strawberry Mountain. Atop this north-south ridge is the "singe zone," the transition between gray dead forest and green live forest. The trees on the west side of the ridge were killed by the 1980 blast, although most were left standing (unlike on Windy Ridge). Boundary Trail No. 1 connects these two ridges.

Boundary Trail No. 1
(Between Forest Roads 26 and 99)

Distance: 1.5 miles to Ghost Lake, 6 miles to Forest
   Road 99 at Bear Meadow
Hiking time: 3 hours for round trip to Ghost Lake, full
   day for round trip to Ghost Lake and Road 99
Difficulty: More difficult
Best time to hike: July through October
Trailhead: Forest Road 26

From the Norway Pass trailhead, Boundary Trail No.
1 extends along the divide between the Lewis and Cispus
rivers for over 40 miles toward Mount Adams. The first
couple of miles of this trail, especially with a side trip
to Ghost Lake, make a good half-day or day-long hike
through the transition zone, where trees killed by the
1980 blast are mixed with live ones.

From Road 26, the trail climbs through downed trees.
At the top of the ridge—which is especially nice at
sunrise and during full moons (complete with hooting
owls)—the trail passes through a scenic bowl of half-
fallen, half-standing snags, then drops into a basin with
occasional islands of old-growth trees. As at Meta Lake,
short trees and plants, protected by a thick snowpack,
survived the 1980 blast. Just past a bridge over a small
creek, red flags mark the future trail to Ghost Lake.

This 0.4-mile-long side trail to captivating Ghost
Lake is presently being constructed. In the meantime, an
unmaintained trail a few yards west of the bridge leads
almost to the lake. This informal trail crosses a large
marsh on a dead tree and passes through an island of
untouched forest. The trail reenters the blast zone and
then fades out in downed trees just as Ghost Lake comes
into view. Hikers must walk along and crawl over huge
logs to reach the lake and its lovely beach, which is

often covered with elk tracks. There are also good views of the Ryan Lake basin. This is an important research area, so please tread lightly.

Past the Ghost Lake turnoff, Boundary Trail No. 1, lined with huckleberry bushes, rises southward out of the basin. If you are on a day hike, the location where the volcano, Cascade Peaks Viewpoint, and Road 99 come into view is a good place to turn around. Past here, the trail becomes steep and sandy and then turns into a "typical" Northwest trail, with green growth everywhere and springs cascading across the pathway. It is 5.5 miles from the Road 26 trailhead to the junction with Strawberry Mountain Trail 220. Boundary Trail No. 1 continues to the right another half-mile to Forest Road 99 at Bear Meadow.

See The Mountaineers' *100 Hikes in the South Cascades and Olympics* for more information on the portion of Boundary Trail No. 1 east of Bear Meadow (where it is open to motorcycles).

Strawberry Mountain Trail 220

Distance: 10 miles total
Hiking time: Short to full-day trips
Difficulty: More difficult
Best time to hike: July through October
Trailheads: Forest Roads 2516, 26, and (via Boundary
   Trail No. 1) 99

Strawberry Mountain Trail 220, which generally follows a ridge that is the border between blast-killed and live forests, is divided into two sections by Road 2516. The southern half of this trail ends at Boundary Trail No. 1 near Bear Meadow (2.5 miles from Road 2516). The northern half of Trail 220 drops down to Road 26 a few miles south of its junction with Road 25 (near Iron Creek); this northern section of the trail is 6.5 miles long. It is generally best to hike the trail (either way) from the trailhead on Road 2516.

To reach the summit of Strawberry Mountain from Road 2516, follow Trail 220 south along a road for 0.25 mile. The trail then goes off the road to the right and climbs steeply for 0.75 mile. At the ridgetop, turn right (north) to reach the 5464-foot summit, where a new fire lookout is planned. Trail 220 provides exceptional vistas as it continues south along the ridge. The trail then drops down the east side of the ridge and enters undamaged conifer forest. Two miles from the summit of Strawberry Mountain, this trail terminates at Boundary Trail No. 1; it is another half-mile to Bear Meadow.

Strawberry Mountain Trail 220 north of Road 2516 is great for short or day-long hikes. It is 6.5 miles to Forest Road 045, a short spur off Road 26. Because the northern end of this trail is in clearcuts, a shuttle to this northern trailhead is probably not worth the effort despite the trail's easy descent as it drops down toward Road 26.

North from Road 2516, Trail 220, with numerous switchbacks, climbs up through live trees to the ridge-top. After dropping into a saddle that has been recently clearcut (and can be very windy and dusty), the trail winds above a hillside of standing but dead trees, which make wonderful foregrounds for the views of the crater and lava dome.

After climbing steeply up a peak, the trail continues north through subalpine meadows that are evolved enough to have paintbrush and harebells. Where the trees killed by the 1980 blast are subalpine trees, groves of stunted snags line the trail. After the trail reenters green forest, it passes high above two lovely small lakes. This is a good place to turn around.

The last third of Strawberry Mountain Trail 220 drops down through classic Northwest forest, including ghost forests of dying trees covered with moss. As the trail leaves the national forest, it enters clearcuts. The rest of the trail was obliterated by logging but was reflagged in 1987. To reach Road 26, you may also follow the logging road (045) downhill over a mile.

Goat Mountain Trail 217

Distance: 5.5 miles to Deadmans Lake, 8.6 miles to upper (Vanson Peak) trailhead
Hiking time: Full day for round trip
Difficulty: More difficult
Best time to hike: July through October
Trailhead: Forest Road 2612 (off Forest Road 26)

Goat Mountain Trail 217—popular with horseback riders—follows a ridge that is the divider between living forest to the north and dead trees, victims of the 1980 blast, to the south. It is a steep climb, but well worth the effort. The panoramic views are stunning, and there is a good spot for a base camp near Deadmans Lake.

It is 5.5 miles to Deadmans Lake—a nice day hike or overnight trip. A one-way trip to Vanson Peak is 7 miles.

To reach the trailhead, turn off Road 26 (0.2 mile north of Ryan Lake) onto Road 2612 and drive 0.4 mile. The Goat Mountain Trail begins through ash in an area that was salvage-logged and burned. (The trailhead has been relocated, as the first part of the old trail was in the blast zone.) The first two miles of the trail climb very steeply through a thick forest of moss-draped firs.

The trail emerges from trees and out on the side of a bald pumice ridge, where it passes by outcrops of granite, patches of huckleberry bushes, and groves of stunted trees. There are many wildflowers and great views of the Green River valley and Mount Rainier (across heavily logged Big Bottom valley), but Mount St. Helens drops behind a ridge as the trail progresses. The trail, above 5000 feet elevation here, crosses to the north side of the ridge and across colorful cliffs and talus slopes before descending into a wooded basin.

Soon after the dusty trail levels out, 5 miles from the trailhead, two side trails to the left (south) lead to

Near the Goat Mountain Trail is a "basket tree," where local Indians cut out a rectangular section of bark to make a basket for collecting berries.

sheltered Deadmans Lake, where there are good camping sites. The trees along the lake's shoreline survived the blast, but there is still a thick layer of ash on the bottom of the clear blue lake.

Just past the side trails to Deadmans Lake, an unmarked trail leads off to the right. This trail (218) leads along a ridge and is being rebuilt to 5250-foot Tumwater Mountain, which is the northern boundary of the Monument. This trail is a nice side excursion if you are camped at Deadmans Lake, but there is no water.

From Deadmans Lake, the main trail continues along a ridgetop, providing great views of Mount Rainier, the upper Green River valley, and the blast zone. A side trail (217A) leads to Vanson Peak (slightly less than 2 miles from Deadmans Lake). Trail 217 ends at a trailhead on Logging Road 2750. (See the Vanson Peak Trails section for more details.)

Green River Trail 213

Distance: Presently 7 miles one way (will be 5 miles)
Hiking time: Full day for round trip
Difficulty: Very strenuous (until trail is cleared)
Best time to hike: June through November
Trailhead: Forest Road 2612 (off Forest Road 26)

To reach the Green River Trail from Road 26, turn west onto Road 2612 a quarter-mile north of Ryan Lake. Follow this gravel road for 3.5 miles. Where Road 2612 turns left to cross the Green River, go straight on an unmarked road as far as you can, which isn't very far if you have a regular car. Then walk down this road, which is just over a mile long. The trail is 7 miles long to Logging Road 2750 near Vanson Peak. This trail is being rebuilt by 1989 and will then be 5 miles long.

At the end of the side road off Road 2612, which is in an area where the trees were killed by the 1980 blast, hikers have to climb over logs for the first half-mile of the trail. The dead trees have been salvage-logged up to the Monument boundary. Then there is a strip of unlogged dead trees that must be crossed. If you have a good sense of balance, it is easiest to walk along downed logs as much as possible—although watch out for loose bark.

When you finally reach green, live trees, angle downhill toward the river until you cross the old trail, which is often hard to follow and requires more bushwhacking than any other trail in the Monument. Numerous downed trees (unrelated to the eruption) block the trail. The new trail, which is flagged, will be higher up the slope to avoid damp areas near the river.

After you reach the Minnie Lee Mine (marked by a sign), the trail markers fade out, but a better trail follows the riverbank. Past the mine, there are numerous excellent camping sites near nice beaches. It is about a 3-

hour round-trip hike to the mine, plus about another hour to the first good camping sites.

Getting to the upper, or western, trailhead for Green River Trail 213 is difficult, a long drive on logging roads that wind out of Morton. The beginning of the access trail (213A) is hard to find, but the logging road that switchbacks down through the clearcut intersects the trail. (See the Vanson Peak Trails section for more details.)

Vanson Peak Trails 217A, 217B, and 217C

Distance: 1.25 miles to Vanson Peak
Hiking time: 2 hours for loop trail
Difficulty: More difficult trail—but very difficult
  trailhead access
Best time to hike: July through October
Trailhead: Logging Road 2750 (from Morton)

It is much shorter and easier to reach Vanson Peak and Vanson Lake from the west instead of via the Goat Mountain Trail (217) from near Ryan Lake. Getting to the trailhead is not that easy, however.

First, follow Highway US-12 east for 5 miles from Morton, then (at milepost 103) turn south on Kosmos Road. At the second intersection (just a short distance), turn left (going straight leads to a boat launch) and follow the road around Riffe Reservoir. Both before and after the road crosses the Cowlitz River, roads lead off to the left, but keep to the right. One mile after the river (5.3 miles from US-12), take the right fork (now called 430), which winds back toward the east. After driving 11.7 miles from US-12, turn left on Logging Road 2600. At the next two forks (miles 13.4 and 14.2), go right. At the next fork (at 15.1 miles), turn left. In 2 miles, this road (2600) intersects Logging Road 2750. Turn left and go a mile to reach the Vanson Peak trailheads; turn right to reach the old Green River trailhead (213A).

The Road 2750 trailheads for Vanson Peak trails 217 and 217C have had to be relocated. The first part of the old Landers Trail No. 217C skirted what became the Monument boundary and was destroyed by Weyerhaeuser's clearcutting in the mid-1980s. The new trailheads are marked with signs and turnouts for parking. The first half-mile of Trail 217 is through a clearcut; Trail 217C is better. (The Monument boundary here is now obvious, as no trees are left standing outside it.)

At 0.75 mile, Trail 217C ends at Trail 217. To the right leads to the Green River Trail. Follow the fork to the left toward Vanson Peak and the lake. A few yards further, there is another fork. The left trail (217A) climbs a half-mile to Vanson Peak, which provides sweeping vistas. The foundations of the old Vanson Peak fire lookout can still be found.

To visit the lake first, follow the right fork (still 217) 0.75 mile to a recently rebuilt side trail (217B) to the right that drops down to Vanson Lake, a beautiful lake lined with reflecting snags. There is an excellent campsite shortly before the trail reaches the lake.

MUDFLOWS AND LAVA FLOWS (SOUTHEAST SLOPE)

The southern slope of Mount St. Helens has been the scene of considerable volcanic activity in the past, such as a large lava flow almost two thousand years ago, but it largely escaped the 1980 eruptions—except the huge mudflows that resulted from melting snow and glaciers. These mudflows, especially those along the Muddy River and Pine Creek, are great for cross-country hikes and ski trips.

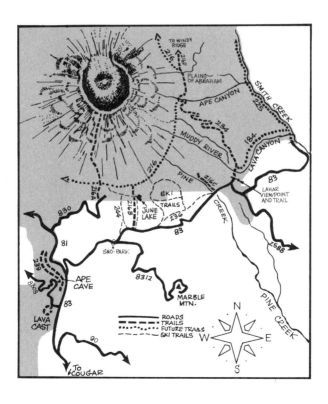

Ape Cave Trail 239

Distance: Lower cave 0.5 mile one way, upper cave 1.5
miles one way (with return trail of 1.25 miles)
Hiking time: Lower cave 2 hours for round trip, upper
cave and return trail half-day for loop trip
Difficulty: More difficult
Best time to hike: April through November
Trailhead: Forest Road 8303 (off Forest Road 83)

Ape Cave is one of many lava tubes buried beneath
the southern slope of Mount St. Helens. The cave is 12,810
feet long and is thought to be the longest lava tube in the
continental United States. Ape Cave Trail is designated
a national recreation trail (as is Boundary Trail No. 1).

The lower cave is an easy hike; the upper section is
more strenuous, requiring a couple of climbs over high
rock piles. Ape Cave can be entered for a short distance
without strong artificial light, but lanterns or similar
light sources are needed to explore very far. You should
bring extra lights. Also the cave is a cool 42° F, so bring a
sweater or jacket. A windbreaker is usually sufficient,
since much of the coolness comes from the constant breeze.

Please be careful while in the cave. Don't leave
trash, smoke cigarettes, or use light sources that produce
smoke, which tarnishes the interior surfaces. Ape Cave
receives so much usage that it is already degraded.

The Forest Service leads interpretive lantern tours
through Ape Cave during the summer. A new interpretive center with book sales and lantern rentals opened in
1989 and is open daily from mid-June through Labor Day,
plus some weekends. The Ape Cave area is closed to
motorized vehicles from December to March because it is
critical winter game habitat. The Forest Service has
additional information on Ape Cave, including a free
brochure, *Ape Cave: A Guide for Exploration.*

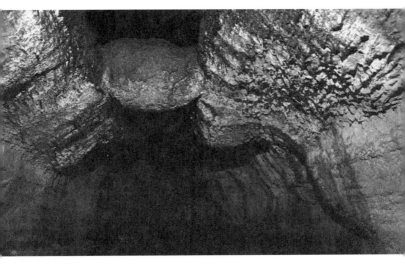

Lower Ape Cave

June Lake Trail 216B

Distance: 1.4 miles one way to June Lake
Hiking time: Half-day for round trip
Difficulty: More difficult
Best time to hike: May through October (plus cross-country skiing in winter)
Trailhead: Forest Road 83

This short feeder trail to Loowit Trail 216 is designed with extra width to be a cross-country ski route. It connects with the Swift Creek cross-country ski trails to make enjoyable loop trips.

The trail follows a creek and climbs gently through second-growth trees. After entering older forest, the trail skirts tiny June Lake, which is located in a notch in a cliff and is fed by a scenic waterfall. The trail continues for another 0.2 mile, terminating at Loowit Trail 216.

Ptarmigan Trail 216A

Distance: 2.1 miles to timberline, 3.9 miles to crater rim
Hiking time: Full day for round trip to summit
Difficulty: More difficult to timberline, very strenuous to summit
Best time to hike: June through October
Trailhead: Forest Road 830 (off Forest Road 81)

In 1987 the south slope, the backside of the volcano, was reopened, allowing climbers the opportunity to climb to the rim and look down on the lava dome in the crater. Ptarmigan Trail 216A is the most popular route, since it begins at a high elevation (3700 feet). The views are spectacular, but the climb up steep pumice and lava slopes is exhausting. Allow 8 to 10 hours for a round trip.

Climbing permits for travel above 4800 feet (about timberline) are required between May 16 and October 31. Climbers are required to register at Yale Park year-round. Climbing permits are good for 36 hours, so climbers can camp near timberline the night before their ascent.

(See *Climbing* in Chapter 3, Visiting the Volcano, for more details on climbing permits.) Warning: The crater rim is unstable and extremely dangerous! Landslides are common, so stay away from the edge.

This is not a difficult climb in

a technical sense, but rather a slow, tiring march up steep slopes. Water is not available above timberline, so bring along adequate liquid to drink. Goggles or sunglasses with side guards can be very important during the all-too-common ash storms atop the mountain, and gaiters can help keep the ever-present ash out of hiking boots.

After 2 huckleberry-lined miles through forest, the Ptarmigan Trail crosses Loowit Trail 216. At 4800-foot timberline, the easy part of the route is over. From here, a "trail" up Monitor Ridge is marked by plastic ribbons on stakes (to be changed). It is a slow, rough climb up soft ash ravines and over rock piles, and there is little shelter from the sun and wind.

By following the tree line to the right at timberline, hikers can work their way down the scoured headwaters of Swift Creek, an area of steep slopes covered with bear grass, small stands of evergreens, and small streams. It is doubtful that you will see other people in this area, but elk are quite plentiful.

For more information on climbing in the Mount St. Helens area, see Fred Beckey's *Cascade Alpine Guide (Vol. I)*, The Mountaineers.

Ape Canyon Trail 234

Distance: 5.5 miles one way to Ape Canyon
Hiking time: Full day for round trip
Difficulty: More difficult
Best time to hike: June through October (also good for
    winter camping—except for snowmobile noise)
Trailhead: Forest Road 83

Trail 234, one of the most spectacular in the Monument, terminates at Loowit Trail 216 near the upper end of Ape Canyon, a deep ravine where there was a reputed Bigfoot sighting in the 1920s (thus the name). By continuing on the Loowit and Abraham trails, hikers can cross the Plains of Abraham and reach Forest Road 99 at Windy Ridge. The trail makes a good overnight trip, but you need to bring water, since the only water available is about the color of chocolate milk.

From Lahar Viewpoint, follow the now-blocked road north across the creek that formed Lava Canyon. Shortly after climbing out of the ravine, Trail 234 leaves the road (to the left where noted by a sign) and begins a steep ascent up a mostly wooded ridge. (The road is going to be extended across the lahar to the trailhead.)

After some open vistas overlooking the Muddy River lahar (mudflow), much of this 5-mile stretch of the trail is sheltered by old-growth trees, including Douglas and noble firs, which are a great contrast to the open, dusty mudflows at the beginning and end of the trail—especially on hot days. On the upper section of the ridge, the trail cuts back and forth, with alternating views of the lahar and the deep Ape Canyon drainage.

The trail exits from the woods for the last time at the breathtaking overlook above Ape Canyon, the lower portion of which has been logged. This slot is cut into 36,000-year-old deposits, the oldest traceable to Mount

St. Helens. Above the trail, along the divide overlooking the lahar, there are a few camping spots. Staying overnight here, while dusty and often hot, allows the cool early-morning exploration of the barren Plains of Abraham. (Warning: Mice are thriving in this less-than-hospitable place.)

Near the Ape Canyon overlook, the trail becomes the Plains of Abraham section of Loowit Trail 216. This trail crosses the stream that cut the deep slot and then climbs up on the Plains and over to the ledge at the top of the waterfall previously visible from the trail. Here one can watch the stream getting larger as the morning sun melts snow and ice further up the volcano, carrying a constant stream of large rocks over the falls. At this stage of change on the side of the volcano, the processes—not just the results—of natural forces can be witnessed. For those who study and photograph the eroding landscape, the year-to-year changes are dramatic.

The section of this trail from the Ape Canyon overlook to Windy Ridge is one of the few sections of the Monument where one feels part of a natural landscape.

Needless to say, some clearcuts and roads are visible in the distance, but on this rugged plateau, one can usually find the backcountry solitude of a large park.

The park that the Plains of Abraham is most reminiscent of is Death Valley, the driest and sparsest of American deserts. As in the desert, this trail can be very hot, and there is virtually no shade during midday. The Death Valley-like stark beauty is apparent in the "painted desert" swaths of pastel colors, especially the lavenders and yellows, above the plateau.

Pine Creek Trail 216C

Distance: 0.4 mile one way to a shelter
Hiking time: 1 hour for round trip
Difficulty: Easiest
Best time to use: Good for cross-country skiing
Trailhead: Forest Road 83

This truncated trail up Pine Creek once went to Ape Canyon and the Plains of Abraham, but the 1980 lahar (mudflow) from Shoestring Glacier destroyed much of it. The trail still provides good access to Pine Creek (beyond the deep ravines) and the mudflow "upstream" from Lahar Viewpoint. There is a shelter on this trail, which makes it good for cross-country skiing.

The trailhead for the Pine Creek Trail is on Forest Road 83 about a half-mile west of the Lahar Viewpoint (just east of the new bridge). From the road, the trail winds through forest for 0.4 mile to the shelter, which sits on the bank above scoured-out Pine Creek. Past the shelter, the trail passes through clearcuts, which allow good views of the volcano, and is marked by blue metal markers on trees, making it easy to follow during winter. The trail suddenly ends at the lahar 0.3 mile from the log shelter.

TOUTLE AND KALAMA RIVERS (SOUTHWEST SLOPE)

The southwest slope of Mount St. Helens has been abused with clearcutting, but some gems remain (or, as often as not, were recreated in 1980) for exploration. The now-solidified but rapidly eroding mudflows down the South Fork Toutle River (opposite page) and Sheep Canyon are especially intriguing. Being on the backside of the crater, shielded from direct blasts, the timberline flora and scenery here are more like those found at other Cascade volcanoes.

Access to some trails is still difficult, and considerable trail construction is in progress. Also, the southwestern slope of the volcano and its trails are very popular with hunters in autumn.

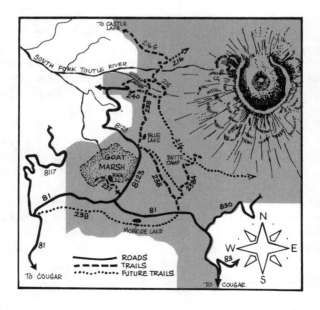

Butte Camp Trail 238A

Distance: 2.7 miles one way to Butte Camp, 3.7 miles to Loowit Trail 216 at timberline
Hiking time: Full day for round trip
Difficulty: More difficult
Best time to hike: June through October (also a winter climbing route)
Trailhead: Forest Road 81

The new trail to Butte Camp passes through many interesting landscapes, including stands of old-growth Douglas fir, noble fir, and lodgepole pine. The open slopes around timberline are exceptionally scenic, but please be careful to minimize disturbance, because this is an important and fragile research area.

This is a popular route for climbers headed to the rim, especially in early spring. A climbing permit is required above 4800 feet. (See *Climbing* in Chapter 3, Visiting the Volcano, for information on obtaining permits.)

The first mile of the hike to Butte Camp is on a section of Toutle Trail 238 that begins at Road 81 near the base of an *aa* (Hawaiian-type) lava flow. The trailhead is located a couple of miles east of Road 81's junction with Forest Road 8123. The trailhead and first part of the trail have been relocated west of the old route (which is now designated for horse use).

The first part of the trail goes across a jumble of rocks, part of a 2000-year-old lava flow, and is easy. At a third of a mile, after the trail enters cut-over forest, the trail splits. The left fork follows an old logging road at first and is old Toutle Trail 238 to Road 8123 and Blue Lake; take the right fork. A mile from the road, there is another junction. The left fork is the new route of Toutle Trail 238 (under construction). The right fork is the beginning of Butte Camp Trail 238A.

At 2.7 miles from Road 81, the trail passes the camp, then continues on a mile uphill to the Loowit Trail. This landscape is easily disturbed, so camping is allowed only at lower Butte Camp (where there is a stream).

Toutle (Blue Lake) Trail 238

Distance: 2.7 miles one way to Sheep Canyon Trail 240,
   4.3 miles to Loowit Trail 216 at the South Fork Toutle
Hiking time: Half-day for round trip to Sheep Canyon,
   full day to include Sheep Canyon loop
Difficulty: More difficult
Best time to hike: June through October
Trailhead: Forest Road 8123

Toutle Trail 238, part of which is presently being rebuilt, provides access to the Sheep Canyon loop for those without vehicles capable of reaching the trailhead at the end of Road 8123. This trail is used by horse parties—and is heavily used by hunters in fall.

The primary trailhead is located where Forest Road 8123 crosses Coldspring Creek just after the road turns to the west 1.7 miles from Forest Road 81. Follow the trail north to reach Blue Lake and Sheep Canyon.

From Road 8123, Trail 238 also heads southeast 3 miles to Road 81 (west of Kalama Springs), where it is the beginning of the trail to Butte Camp. This section is being relocated to a higher elevation, and in the future, Trail 238 will be extended south of Road 81 past McBride Lake and along the Kalama River to the old work center.

North of Road 8123, the Toutle Trail follows the creek and at 0.2 mile passes above Blue Lake, a small but scenic lake formed when a lahar dammed the creek (a nice place to have lunch). The trail then climbs gently through one of largest stands of noble firs left in the world, passes through a clearcut, and finally drops into Sheep Canyon. Mudflows down Sheep Creek wiped out a section of the old Toutle Trail, but the trail now crosses the new Sheep Canyon Trail 240 and then crosses the Sheep Canyon mudflow (where a bridge is being built) to drop into the South Fork Toutle River valley.

Sheep Canyon Trail 240

Distance: 2 miles to Loowit Trail, 6.8 miles for loop hike
Hiking time: Full day for loop trail
Difficulty: More difficult
Best time to hike: June through October
Trailhead: Forest Road 8123

Trail 240 is part of the Sheep Canyon loop, which also includes sections of the Toutle and Loowit trails. This spectacular loop trail, which planners designed to be hiked counterclockwise, passes through many diverse examples of volcanism.

This trail begins at the end of Road 8123, where there is also a quarter-mile trail to a viewpoint overlooking the South Fork Toutle River, Sheep Canyon, and a nice stand of noble fir. At present, however, vehicles with considerable power and clearance are required to reach the trailhead, plus the end of the road is sometimes closed during hunting season. This road is going to be relocated to make access easier. Meanwhile, it is best to stop at the turnaround 5.7 miles from Road 81 and walk ahead to see if you think you can make the steep turn where Road 8123 turns sharply to the right (and a timber-company road to the left drops into the Toutle valley). If you can't make it, the trail is over a mile longer. Toutle Trail 238 can also be used to reach Sheep Canyon.

At the Sheep Canyon trailhead, follow the trail a half-mile upstream. Just past a rock that provides a great view of a waterfall, a trail (238) cuts off to the left and drops down to cross Sheep Creek; this is the return trail of the loop. Continue straight ahead up the drainage past another junction with Trail 238 (to Blue Lake).

The next trail junction (another 1.5 miles) is the end of Trail 240 at Loowit Trail 216. The right fork (toward the mountain) is under construction and will tie into the Butte

Camp Trail 2.1 miles away. A short side trip up this section of the Loowit Trail is recommended, as over the next ridge the trail drops into a deep ravine reminiscent of Mount Rainier's glacial moraines.

The left fork, the continuation of the loop, follows a ridge with vegetation evolved beyond that on most other Mount St. Helens slopes. Of all the Monument trails, this section is most like a traditional Northwest "volcano" hike. It even smells right! As the trail winds between lupine-carpeted meadows and stunted subalpine forests, the views of Mount St. Helens are stunning.

On a ledge above the barren South Fork Toutle River streambed (2.7 miles from the end of Sheep Canyon Trail 240), the Loowit Trail intersects with the end of Toutle Trail 238. The right fork is the Loowit continuation and leads to a side trail (216G) presently being completed along a ridge to Castle Lake, about 6 miles away. The trail to the left (240) is the loop trail and passes through lush forest practically undisturbed by the 1980 eruption. The forest floor is carpeted with sorrel and ferns, and vine maple is abundant, making autumn especially colorful. There is even a good campsite near a stream. It is 1.6 miles back to the Sheep Canyon Trail.

Goat Marsh Trail 237

Distance: 1 mile one way to lake
Hiking time: 2 hours round trip
Difficulty: Easiest
Best time to hike: May through
November
Trailhead: Forest Road 8123

Trail 237 is an easy hike through forest to a lake and marsh protected (except from hunting) within the 1000-acre Goat Marsh Research Natural Area, which is nestled in a basin between 4965-foot Goat Mountain and the Butte Camp Dome extrusion on Mount St. Helens. Fed by Coldspring Creek, this oasis amid clearcuts is populated with elk, waterfowl, and other wildlife and is the largest and most important wetland habitat in the Monument. Part of the peaceful lake is covered with water lilies, which provide good habitat for frogs and are especially photogenic when in bloom.

It is 1 mile to the lake and another half-mile to the marsh. This near-level trail may have to be relocated due to continual abuses by ORV users. Mosquitos are common in summer—as are hunters in autumn.

To reach the trailhead, which has parking for two vehicles, turn north off Forest Road 81 onto Road 8123 and drive 0.6 mile. The first part of the trail follows a closed road, then turns right at an old quarry. The trail enters the research area at a log fence intended to keep

out motorbikes and snowmobiles.

After reaching the lake, the trail follows the shoreline, providing access to viewpoints with the volcano
reflecting in the lake. After the trail leaves the marsh,
it is blocked by fallen logs. An unmaintained trail continues on to the talus slopes at the base of Goat Mountain,
which is very steep but provides excellent vistas.

Loowit Trail 216 and Future Trails

The U.S. Forest Service is presently working on the construction of the remaining segments of Loowit Trail 216, also called the 'Round-the-Mountain Trail. When completed in the early 1990s, this trail will be almost 30 miles long and will cross the pumice plain in front of the crater and Loowit Falls (the last section to be built, in part to protect research areas).

At present, portions of this trail are completed on the western and eastern slopes and tie into feeder trails, such as the ones to Ape Canyon and Sheep Canyon. Like the Wonderland Trail around Mount Rainier, the Loowit Trail will wind in and out of forests near timberline, with open meadows providing spectacular (though neck straining) views of the volcano.

In addition to the remaining portions of Loowit Trail 216, numerous other trails are being built at St. Helens:

The trail (225) up Smith Creek, beginning at its confluence with the Muddy River below Lava Canyon, is under construction. When completed, it will extend to Forest Road 99 (the Donnebrook Viewpoint near Windy Ridge Viewpoint) about 6 miles away. From a geologic standpoint, many scientists consider the route up Smith Creek the most interesting in the Monument.

When completed, the trail down Lava Canyon (184) from near Lahar Viewpoint will be one of the finest at Mount St. Helens. The Muddy River mudflow that resulted from the melting of Shoestring Glacier scoured out Lava Canyon, exposing dramatic lava formations. The first part of the trail will be a barrier-free boardwalk to the top of a waterfall spilling over a basalt cliff. When completed, this trail will connect to the beginning of the Smith Creek Trail. Among the features that will be easily accessible then is the Ship, a 150-foot-high lava monolith rising out of the canyon.

As more of the landscape around Mount St. Helens is opened to the public and more trails are completed, this guide will expand to accommodate the additions. Your suggestions, which will be greatly appreciated, can be sent to: Chuck Williams, c/o Elephant Mountain Arts, P.O. Box 902, White Salmon, WA 98672.

INDEX

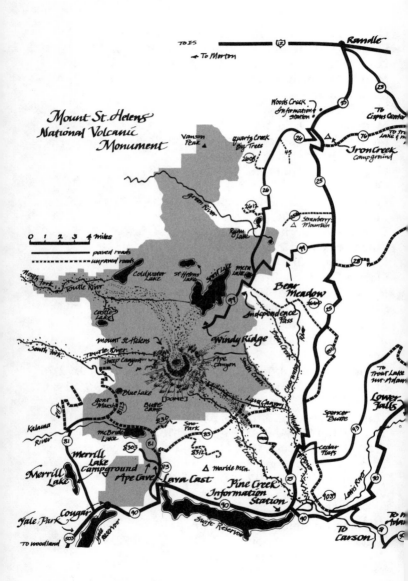

Mount St. Helens
National Volcanic
Monument

TO ES
← To Morton

Randle

Woods Creek
Information
Station

To Cispus Center

Vanson Peak

Quartz Creek
Big Trees

Iron Creek
Camp ground

TO ST.
LAKE & M.

Green River

Ryan Lake

Strawberry
Mountain

0 1 2 3 4 miles

—— paved roads
----- unpaved roads

North Fork
Toutle River

Coldwater Lake

St Helens
Lake

Spirit Lake

Meta Lake

Bear
Meadow

Castle Lake

Independence Pass

South Fork
Toutle River

Mount St Helens

Windy Ridge

Sheep Canyon

Ape Canyon

South Fork

To Trout Lake
Mt. Adams

Blue Lake

[DOME]

Lava Canyon

Goat Marsh

Butte Camp

Sno-Park

Spencer Butte

Lower Falls

Kalama River

McBride Lake

Marble Mtn.

Cedar Flats

Merrill Lake
Campground

Ape Cave

Lava Cast

Pine Creek
Information
Station

Merrill Lake

Lewis River

To M.
Adams

Yale Park

Cougar

Yale Reservoir

Swift Reservoir

To Carson

TO Woodland

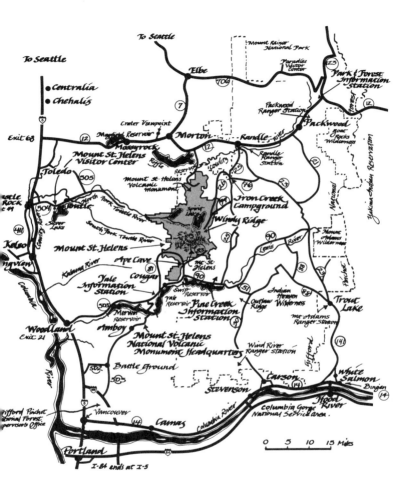

ABOUT THE AUTHOR: Chuck Williams is a free-lance writer and photographer from the Columbia Gorge. He is the author/photographer of *Bridge of the Gods, Mountains of Fire: A Return to the Columbia Gorge*; the author of *Mount St. Helens: A Changing Landscape*; and a contributor to *Progress As If Survival Mattered* and *Western Water Made Simple*. His articles and photographs have appreared in numerous publications, including *Audubon*, *Sierra*, and *High Country News*. He is Cascade Indian and the newsletter editor for the Columbia River Inter-Tribal Fish Commission, the fisheries agency for the Nez Perce, Umatilla, Warm Springs, and Yakima tribes.

Williams is a long-time activist in the environmental movement. He is the former national parks expert for Friends of the Earth, is a cofounder of the Columbia Gorge Coalition (the group that began the campaign for a Columbia Gorge National Scenic Area), and was instrumental in the efforts to protect the Klickitat and White Salmon rivers as wild-and-scenic rivers and to designate Indian Heaven and Trapper Creek as wilderness areas.

SPECIAL THANKS TO: My mother Bettye, my father Clyde, and my family; Kim Arfsten; Susan Saul, Noel McCrae, and the Mount St. Helens Protective Association; Tim Wapato, Laura Berg, and everyone at the Columbia River Inter-Tribal Fish Commission for their patience; Dick Adlard, Sue Hall, David Thies, and all the wonderful Gorge residents who helped; Bill Kaiser, Bill McMillan, and the Gifford Pinchot Task Force; Don Swanson and the U.S. Geological Survey; Frank James; and all the U.S. Forest Service personnel who helped, including Francisco Valenzuela, Jim Gale, Jim Quiring, Larry Schumacher, Stephen Nofield, Thom Corcoran, Barbara Hollenbeck, and others too numerous to name.